TOSCANA MIA

TOSCANA

Photographed in Tuscany by
PAOLO BONSIGNORI

MIA

The Heart and Soul of Tuscan Cooking

UMBERTO MENGHI

Douglas & McIntyre
Vancouver/Toronto/New York

Douglas & McIntyre Ltd.
2323 Quebec Street, Suite 201
Vancouver, British Columbia V5T 4S7

Canadian Cataloguing in Publication Data
Menghi, Umberto, 1946–
   Toscana Mia
   Includes index.
   ISBN 1-55054-721-6
   1. Cookery, Italian—Tuscan style. I. Title.
TX723.2.T86M44 2000   641.5945′5   C00-910792-4

   Library of Congress Cataloging-in-Publication Data
Menghi, Umberto, 1946–
   Toscana Mia : the heart and soul of Tuscan cooking / Umberto Menghi ;
   photographed in Tuscany by Paolo Bonsignori
        p. cm.
   Includes index.
   ISBN 1-55054-721-6 (alk. paper)
   1. Cookery, Italian—Tuscan style. I. Title.

   TX723.2.T86M46 2001
   641.5945′5–dc21   00-060238

Editing by Elizabeth Wilson
Design and typesetting by Praxis
Front jacket photograph by Kate Williams
Interior photographs by Paolo Bonsignori
Additional photographs by Rob Melnychuk, pages 12-13 and 15, and back jacket
Translation by Anneliese Schultz
Metric conversion by Darlene Grant
Printed and bound in Canada by Friesens
Printed on acid-free paper

We gratefully acknowledge the financial support of the Canada Council for the Arts,
the British Columbia Ministry of Tourism, Small Business and Culture, and the
Government of Canada through the Book Publishing Industry Development Program
(BPIDP) for our publishing activities.

ACKNOWLEDGEMENTS

WRITING TOSCANA MIA has brought back the memories of childhood and of the ways of *mi amici toscani*, my Tuscan friends.

I must first thank Mom and Dad. My direction came from them, and as I was writing, I had their spirits next to me, helping me to think about all they taught me. All the Tuscan places I've visited, they took me to first.

This book is also dedicated to what we do at Villa Delia. My two sisters, Marietta and Giuliana, are very much involved with me in the cooking school, helping to keep alive the things we learned in our family kitchen. Villa Delia exists so the world can come and experience the Tuscan adventure. My investor friends made all this possible.

My wife, Marian, and my son, Alessandro, deserve special thanks for all the time they spent waiting for me when I was spending so many hours on this book.

Elizabeth Wilson was my editor; without all her patience and help this book would not have come together. Designer Roberto Dosil went over to Tuscany to lend his vision to the photography, then came home and wove the photos and text together in a way that makes this book very special. Photographer Paolo Bonsignori shares with me the same emotions about his home. With Roberto, then with me, Paolo travelled tirelessly around the province to capture the uniquely Tuscan moments that enhance the stories and recipes. Vancouver photographer Kate Williams made me smile while we were shooting. And the people at Douglas & McIntyre believed in me. My appreciation to all.

To all my staff and chefs, thank you for your help, understanding and support.

Once again, I must mention my angel, my sister Marietta and her husband, Silvano Malacarne, who have given me such technical support in operating Villa Delia. Everything comes together for me in our Villa. Our mother found it; Marietta and I get to work there, and we have the privilege of sharing our Tuscany with the world.

FOOD AND WINE

I have asked my friend Anthony Gismondi to walk through Tuscany with me and suggest wines of the region that best accompany some of the recipes. This man has a passion for wines and a deep foundation of knowledge, which he constantly builds upon by visiting producers and wine regions around the world.

Tony is Canada's most influential wine critic. If you fly Air Canada, you will be served wines that he has selected. He is the wine columnist for the *National Post*, the *Vancouver Sun*, *Vancouver Magazine* and *CityFood Magazine*. He is the Senior West Coast Editor at *Wine Access-Canada's Essential Guide to Wine and Spirits*, and Canadian Editor of *Oz Clarke's Wine Guide* on CD-ROM and *Oz Clarke's Pocket Wine Book 2000*. He also co-hosts the lively "Food and Wine Show" on Vancouver's CFUN Radio.

The wines he suggests in these pages are all Tuscan, and some may not be easily available where you live, but Tony's explanations of the qualities of the selected wines will make it possible for you to find others with similar attributes which will enhance these dishes.

I have followed Tony's guidance on wines for many years and have always respected his opinions. I can't think of a better person to give us advice. *Grazie*, Tony.

Contents

From
D AVANTI S AN - G UIDO
Giosuè Carducci

I cipressi che a Bólgheri alti e schietti
Van da San Guido in duplice filar,

Quasi in corsa giganti giovinetti
Mi balzarono incontro e mi guardâr,

Mi riconobbero, e – Ben torni omai –
Bisbigliaton vèr me co 'l capo chino –
Perché non scendi? perché non ristai?

Fresca è la sera e a te noto il cammino.

la terra sotto le scarpe

My Home, My Heritage

NOT MANY TUSCANS LEAVE HOME. I did, but as we say, *la terra sotto le scarpe*, the earth sticks to my shoes. Toscana mia, my Tuscany, keeps calling me back. A few years ago my family and friends and I restored a farmhouse in the ancient village of Ripoli. We named it *Villa Delia*, after my mother, and run it as an inn and cooking school, where, I confess, I find myself spending more and more time.

I feel energy in Tuscany. The colours are clear and strong. Aromas fill the air. A famous poem by Giosue Carducci talks about cypress trees seeming to bend toward the one who returns to say welcome. This is my home, my heritage. Is it possible to capture the essence of all that in a cookbook?

First of all, this is more than a collection of recipes. To a Tuscan, food is not just something to eat, it's the very core of life. It is a sense of time, of place, of family – a sense of belonging. We truly believe that we are what we eat.

Over the centuries Tuscans have fought many, many wars to keep this land as it is, for the simple reason that we have found contentment. Everything we need is here. Tuscany embraces the sea and basks in warm winds from the Sahara. As the land climbs towards the mountains, the different soils and climates create varied growing regions. With a little sweat, we can grow almost anything. Out of this comes a passion for agriculture. The people of Tuscany have always seen wealth in terms of land, not money.

I think that attachment to the soil has shaped our character. A Tuscan is basically a very simple person: warm, poetic, passionate and homey. In a world where everything becomes a melting pot, here you find people still enjoying centuries-old microcultures; a kind of city-state mentality has prevailed throughout our history. Each city or town has kept its own flavour . . . and flavours. With this experience and background we are open to new things, but we don't change for the sake of changing. When we adopt something new, it must fit in with a treasured way of life.

Food has always played a central role in our lives. In 800 BC Etruscan nobles were hunting wild boars and roasting them with berries. The aristocratic Catherine de Medici of Florence married the King Henry III of France in the 1500s, and enriched French cooking with the traditions of her homeland.

But good food has never been restricted to the nobility. *Cucina povera*, poor-man's food, is the age-old foundation. It is the clean taste of Tuscany, built on seasonal ingredients at their peak of flavour, aromatics that grow just outside the door and straightforward preparations that let the flavours come through. We have always made the most of what we have whenever we have it.

When you work with simplicity, the ingredients become very important. I must pay respect to the farmers' profound contributions to Tuscan cuisine. Everybody claims to have the best – *My basil is sweeter*; *My rabbits feed on grapes*; *My olive oil is fruitier* . . . Good ingredients, good basics and deep respect for the food make a better dish.

For this book I have searched out the very best, and I offer it to you as Tuscans offer their homemade bread or wine – from the heart. I feel a pride and a responsibility to show where these dishes belong in our land and our history. I will give you recipes, yes, but more than that, I want to give you, from all the Tuscan hearts, an understanding of the energy, the colours, the aromas and the passion that are at work in each one. With that understanding you can put yourself into these dishes and share them with friends and family in the Tuscan spirit of contentment and companionship. To love Tuscany is to love life.

From
PASSING SAN GUIDO
Giosuè Carducci

The tall true cypresses which run
from San Guido to Bolgheri in double file,

Like youthful giants almost raced,
sprang toward me, observed,

Then recognized my face, and "Welcome
back at last," they murmured with heads
bowed. "Why not alight? Why not stay
once again?

The evening's cool, inviting; and you
know the path."

to love Tuscany is to love life

The Land Itself

To travel through the mountains and hills from the plain to the coastline, through the many quiet villages, castles, villas, ruins and palaces, is to experience a tapestry of climates and cultures. The simplicity and richness of the food, its profound aromas and variety are tied to the land itself.

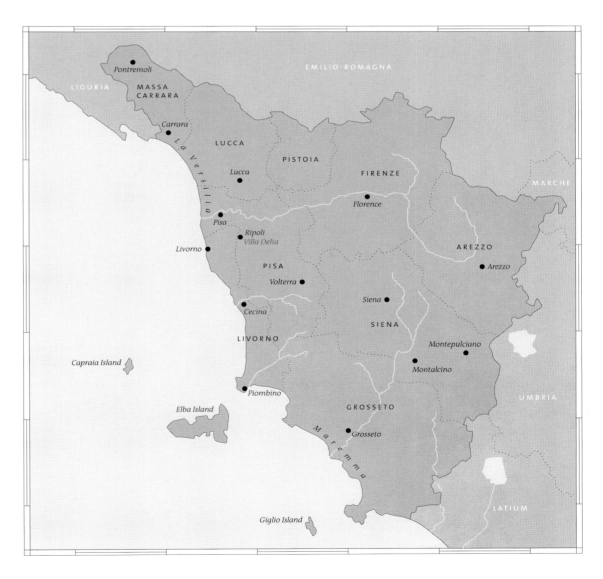

The antipasto is a reason to get together.
You don't say "Let's go for a drink," you say "Let's break bread together."

ANTIPASTI

WARM BEANS WITH CALAMARI

Everybody who comes to Villa Delia loves this elegant and refreshing summer dish. This is classic terra e mare *– land and sea. The flavour of the earth is in the fruity beans, the flavour of the sea is in the calamari, and they're brought together by nutty arugula and chili-tinged olive oil. Serve this on its own or as a complement to steamed fish.*

INGREDIENTS

SPICY OLIVE OIL

1/2 cup [125 mL]	extra virgin olive oil
1 tsp [5 mL]	hot red pepper flakes
1 lb [500 g]	dried cannellini (white kidney) beans
1 Tbsp [15 mL]	salt
1 sprig	rosemary
1	sage leaf
4 cloves	garlic, whole
1/2 lb [250 g]	calamari
1 Tbsp [15 mL]	olive oil
	salt and pepper
	juice of 1 lemon
1 bunch	arugula, washed, dried and stemmed (about a handful per person)

SERVES 4

PREPARATION

For the spicy olive oil, marinate the pepper flakes in the oil for a minimum of 4 hours, but no more than 6 hours. Strain out the flakes and discard them.

Soak the beans in cold water for a minimum of 8 hours. Drain the water and put the beans in about 12 cups [3 L] of lightly salted fresh water. Add rosemary, fresh sage and whole garlic cloves (not chopped!).

Bring to a boil, reduce the heat to low and boil gently for 1 hour, covered. Beans should be cooked al dente. Strain the beans in a colander and transfer them to a bowl. Drizzle on the spicy oil and keep the beans warm.

Clean the calamari and cut them into 1/4 in. [5 mm] rings. Heat the olive oil over medium heat and sauté the calamari quickly for 2 minutes. Season with salt and pepper. Remove the calamari rings from the oil and blot with paper towels. Add the calamari to the beans. Squeeze the lemon juice onto the mixture. Adjust the seasoning with salt and pepper.

Serve lukewarm on a bed of fresh arugula.

PICKLED VEGETABLES

You will always find these pickled vegetables on an antipasto platter. They're usually served with a drizzle of extra virgin olive oil. My aunt preserves the whole recipe in one large jar, but smaller jars will do just fine. Use the freshest possible vegetables for best results.

INGREDIENTS

1 lb [500 g]	carrot
1 lb [500 g]	onions
1 lb [500 g]	zucchini
1 lb [500 g]	fennel
1 lb [500 g]	cauliflower florets
1 lb [500 g]	cucumber
1 lb [500 g]	celery
1 lb [500 g]	bell pepper
16 cups [4 L]	white vinegar
1 2/3 cups [400 mL]	extra virgin olive oil
2 cups [500 mL]	non-iodized coarse salt (kosher or pickling salt)
2 cups [500 mL]	sugar

MAKES 10 QUARTS [10 L]

PREPARATION

Wash all the vegetables and trim them as required. Cut them into finger-sized pieces. You will end up with about 2 cups [500 mL] of each when they're cut.

Bring vinegar, oil, salt and sugar to a boil. Add the vegetables and boil for 5 minutes.

Put vegetables and liquid into sterilized glass canning jars. Seal the jars according to manufacturer's directions. Process them in boiling water for 20 minutes (no longer).

Remove the jars from the water and let them cool. Store them in a dark, cool place until needed.

MUSHROOM CARPACCIO

This is simplicity at its best: mushrooms, good Parmesan cheese and olive oil, fresh herbs and a couple of piquant accents. I usually use fresh porcini or champignon mushrooms. Any size will do, but larger ones are less work. You could embellish this dish with some shaved white truffle if you happen to be in the right place at the right time, but it's hardly necessary.

INGREDIENTS

1/2 lb [250 g]	porcini or champignon mushrooms
	salt
	freshly ground black pepper
	juice of 1/2 lemon
2–3 dashes	Tabasco sauce
	extra virgin olive oil
5–6 shavings	Parmesan cheese per person
1 sprig	parsley, finely chopped
	handful of arugula, optional

SERVES 4

PREPARATION

Brush the mushrooms clean and remove the stems. Slice the caps vertically as thinly as possible: a mandoline or vegetable slicer works well. Place the slices in one layer on a serving platter. Sprinkle with salt and pepper. Squeeze the half lemon into a cup and add Tabasco to taste. Sprinkle the juice over the mushrooms. The lemon juice "cooks" and tenderizes the mushrooms.

Drizzle the oil evenly over the mushrooms. Using a vegetable peeler, shave the Parmesan on top, and sprinkle with parsley. If you wish, scatter a handful of arugula over the mushrooms. Serve immediately.

STUFFED CHILIES

Am I getting older? I never cared for chilies when I was a kid, but my father loved them and took special care growing them. He would eat them any time, any way. Now I understand why. As a cocktail party appetizer or as part of an antipasto platter, these little morsels are always a hit. They can also be served as a main dish topped with a fonduta di pomodoro *(see page 63) and served on a bed of rice.*

INGREDIENTS

12	mild fresh yellow or green chilies (jalapeños or Hungarian wax chilies work well)
1/4 lb [125 g]	lean ground meat (any beef or poultry will work)
1 Tbsp [15 mL]	finely chopped sundried tomato
1 Tbsp [15 mL]	chopped basil
1 Tbsp [15 mL]	chopped mint
1 Tbsp [15 mL]	coriander leaves (cilantro)
1 Tbsp [15 mL]	crushed pine nuts
6 cloves	garlic, minced
1	egg
	salt
	freshly ground black pepper
	oil for deep frying
1/2 cup [125 mL]	flour
1/2–2/3 cup [125–150 mL]	ice water
	flour for dusting

SERVES 6 AS AN APPETIZER

PREPARATION

Wash the chilies. Without splitting them in half, slit one side and scrape out the seeds and ribs.

In a bowl, combine the ground meat, sundried tomato, herbs, pine nuts, garlic, egg and salt and pepper to taste. Mix well. Use a small spoon or a pastry bag to fill the chilies with the meat mixture.

Pour 2 in. [5 cm] of oil into a medium pot and heat it to hot.

Mix the flour with enough ice water to make a thin batter. Dust the chilies with flour, then dip them into the batter and coat well.

Slide the chilies one by one into the hot oil, being careful not to crowd the pot, and fry about 3 to 4 minutes, turning from time to time. When they're golden brown all over, lift the chilies out with a slotted spoon and drain well on paper towels. Serve them when they are still warm.

VILLA DELIA

A little over a decade ago, two women shared a hospital room. As they found the strength to talk, they discovered they had a lot in common. Both of them had spent their married lives on family farms. Both had seen their children abandon farming, moving on to other, more prosperous places to make a living.

FOR ONE, THE VINEYARDS she and her husband had worked so hard to maintain had been sold as a housing estate. For the other, the farm, with its collapsing roofs and crumbling walls, would soon suffer the same fate because no one could afford to maintain it.

They commiserated. Both hoped that the way of life they treasured so much would not die, and yet both saw how things were changing in the modern world. Children everywhere were abandoning the family estate so they could work in the city.

At some point, one of them, Delia, made a suggestion. Her son had left Tuscany, but now he was coming back often. He had gone to North America and done well in the restaurant business. Now he was coming to appreciate his Tuscan roots, and wanting to return in some way. Perhaps he could buy this other woman's rundown old farm and bring it to life again. It was just an idea. Or maybe it was just a dream.

I am Delia's son. I had a dream too. I had left Tuscany in the 1960s, eager to work hard and prove myself. I saw worlds to conquer. Using my Tuscan traditions as a base, I celebrated Italian cuisine in restaurant after restaurant. My taste and timing were right; I worked hard and became successful.

I was of the generation that had to explore and experiment. The smells and tastes I grew up with were fine; they were a jumping-off point, but with a little originality couldn't I do better? For a long time I thought so.

After a while, my trips back home started to haunt me. A twenty-minute walk in a field gave me as much pleasure as a day driving my Ferrari on a superhighway. The smell of woodsmoke wrenched me back to my childhood and the food I ate then. I began to take the time to walk, seeing the colours and shapes and jarring my memories awake as I inhaled the scents of herbs, grasses and flowers.

I began to understand that the success of Tuscany's food comes directly out of the land and the seasons – that the simplicity of it does not come from laziness, but from an appreciation of what works. I looked at the way the people lived and the way I had grown up, and saw that it all made perfect sense. The more I realized it, the more I wanted to explore the Tuscan ways, study them and share them with the world. I dreamed of going back.

I told my mother of my dream. She told her hospital roommate. I bought the woman's farm, with help from investors and family, and we rebuilt its 54 acres into a gracious country inn and cooking school. My sister Marietta and her husband, Silvano, live there and manage it. Marietta and I give cooking classes together whenever I can be there. We grow olives and grapes and bottle our own oil and wine. And visitors come from all over the world to ease into the Tuscan way of life. It is my greatest pleasure to share with them the essential Tuscan truth of letting nature take its course.

My mother did not live to see the day when the sale was complete and work on the inn began.

We named it after her: Villa Delia.

Silvano and Marietta

CHICKEN LIVER CROSTINI

These rich little bites can be found, warm or cold, on any antipasto platter in Tuscany. If you're expecting a crowd, the recipe can be doubled. It also keeps well in the refrigerator or freezer, so it can be made ahead of time.

INGREDIENTS

11 oz [350 g]	chicken livers, membranes removed
1	medium onion, coarsely chopped
1 stalk	celery with leaves, coarsely chopped
2 cloves	garlic, coarsely chopped
1/2 cup [125 mL]	2-day-old bread, broken up
1 branch	rosemary, leaves removed
	small handful of sage leaves
	small handful of parsley
1/2 cup [125 mL]	classic meat broth *(see page 159)*
4 Tbsp [60 mL]	dry white wine
2 Tbsp [30 g]	butter
2 Tbsp [30 mL]	extra virgin olive oil
3 Tbsp [45 mL]	capers
3	anchovy fillets
	freshly ground black pepper
12–16 slices	Tuscan loaf or baguette, crisped but not toasted

SERVES 6

PREPARATION

Place chicken livers, onion, celery, garlic, bread chunks, rosemary, sage and parsley in a heavy-bottomed pot over medium heat and cook covered for 10 minutes, stirring occasionally.

Add the broth and cook covered another 30 minutes. Add the wine and leave the pot uncovered until the liquid has evaporated.

Remove from heat and put the mixture in a food processor with the butter, oil, capers and anchovies. Process to a smooth, moist spread and stir in pepper to taste.

Spread on crisped bread and serve warm or cold. This spread keeps well in the refrigerator or freezer.

SMOKED SALMON CROSTINI; HAM CROSTINI

Just a reminder that appetizers don't have to be complicated. With these two delicious crostini, your food processor does most of the work. Serve them as cocktail party canapés or as elements of an antipasto platter.

INGREDIENTS

SMOKED SALMON CROSTINI

4 oz [125 g]	smoked salmon
6 Tbsp [80 mL]	unsalted butter (2/3 stick)
1/3 cup [75 mL]	fresh, mild goat cheese or freshly grated Parmesan cheese
1 Tbsp [15 mL]	chopped fresh dill
	juice of 1 lemon
	OR 1 drop of Tabasco sauce
12 slices	wholewheat baguette, cut 1/2 in. [1 cm] thick
6	pitted black olives, cut in half, for garnish

HAM CROSTINI

1/2 cup [125 mL]	cooked ham, not smoked
1/2 cup [125 mL]	unsalted butter
1/2 cup [125 mL]	freshly grated Parmesan cheese
1 Tbsp [15 mL]	extra virgin olive oil
1 tsp [5 mL]	chili-infused oil
	salt
	crushed black pepper
12 slices	wholewheat baguette, cut 1/2 in. [1 cm] thick

EACH SERVES 4 TO 6

PREPARATION

In a food processor, blend the salmon or ham, butter, cheese and flavourings into a fine paste. Spread the paste on the bread slices. The bread can be toasted or not, according to your preference.

Garnish the salmon crostini with olive halves.

WARM CAMBOZOLA WITH CROSTINI

In the crostini family, this is one of my most successful dishes for entertaining. I call it my Lego dish: I can combine the elements in different ways as the need arises – the crostini and cheese on a tray for a cocktail party, or the salad-crostini-cheese combination as a starter or a light lunch with a glass of wine.

INGREDIENTS

6 cloves	garlic, skin on, not separated
	olive oil
	salt
	freshly ground black pepper
8 slices	fresh French bread, cut on the bias about 1/4 in. [5 mm] thick
6	medium tomatoes
	small handful of organic mixed greens per person
1 Tbsp [15 mL]	extra virgin olive oil
1 Tbsp [15 mL]	balsamic vinegar
8 oz [250 g] round	Cambozola

SERVES 4

PREPARATION

Preheat the oven to 350°F [180°C].

To roast the garlic, place the garlic cloves on a piece of foil. Drizzle them with a bit of olive oil and sprinkle with salt and pepper. Wrap the garlic loosely in the foil and roast for 35 to 40 minutes, or until the garlic gives a bit when pressed. Squeeze the garlic out of the skin and chop it finely. (If you want more roasted garlic for another use, cut the top off an entire head of unpeeled garlic, then proceed the same way. It will take more time.)

Set the broiler to 375°F [190°C]. Toast the bread under the broiler until it is lightly browned. Set aside. Leave the broiler on.

Slice the tomatoes in half crosswise. Extract the juice and seeds and discard. Cut the tomatoes in a small dice. Mix the diced tomato with the chopped garlic. Place the mixture on the toasted bread slices.

Toss the greens with oil and vinegar in a bowl. Set the greens in the middle of a large plate. Arrange the tomato crostini around the outside of the plate.

Slice the Cambozola vertically into 4 slices. Lay the slices on a baking sheet and place under the broiler for about 1 minute, or until just softened. Lift the Cambozola slices onto the salad and serve immediately.

DEEP-FRIED CAULIFLOWER

These hot, crispy wedges of cauliflower will disappear quickly, whether you serve them as part of an antipasto platter or as a vegetable side dish. It's hard to say how many they will serve – anywhere from one to eight.

INGREDIENTS

1 head	cauliflower, whole
	salt
	olive oil for frying
3	eggs, beaten
1 cup [250 mL]	milk
1/2 cup [125 mL]	flour
1 cup [250 mL]	tomato sauce *(see page 164)*

SERVES 1 TO 8

PREPARATION

Trim the leaves from the cauliflower but leave it whole. Bring a large pot of salted water to a boil. Place the cauliflower in the pot and cook it until the stalks and florets are tender.

Remove the cauliflower from the water and drain. Cut it in half, slicing vertically through the stalk. Cut the cauliflower into 2 in. [5 cm] wedges.

Pour 1 in. [2.5 cm] of oil into a sauté pan and heat it over medium heat.

In a bowl, mix the beaten eggs with the milk and flour to create a liquid paste. Dip the cauliflower wedges into the paste to coat. Fry them a few at a time in the hot oil until they are crisp and brown on both sides. Drain them on paper towels and keep them warm.

Heat the tomato sauce in another pan and toss it with the cauliflower just before serving.

Soups

A soup at times represents the whole meal,
but it's so rich, so full – a true, bountiful expression of the season.

Puréed Vegetable Soup with Parmesan Foam

Piero Antinori's family has been making wines in Tuscany since 1385. He was the first of the Super Tuscans and loves to try new ways of doing things. When he visited us, we wanted to find an elegant and unusual treatment for the traditional tastes. This is the vegetable equivalent of cappuccino. Use mixed vegetables of the season, such as beans, peas, carrots, celery, zucchini, fennel, tomatoes, broccoli, cauliflower or onions. For the foam, use the best Parmesan you can find.

Ingredients

2 lbs [1 kg]	mixed fresh vegetables, peeled and seeded
2	large potatoes, peeled
2 cloves	garlic, chopped
	handful of basil leaves
	handful of parsley
1 cup [250 mL]	vegetable stock, as needed
	salt
	freshly ground black pepper
	dash of chili-infused oil
	paprika
1 cup [250 mL]	milk
1/4 cup [60 mL]	freshly grated Parmesan cheese

Serves 8

Preparation

Chop the vegetables, potatoes and garlic into a small dice. Place them in a stock pot and cover with twice as much water. Add the basil and parsley. Bring the water to a boil, then reduce it to a simmer. Cook the vegetables until they are very soft: almost, but not quite, falling apart.

Pass the vegetables and liquid through a food mill, or use the back of a wooden spoon to press them through a fine sieve to remove the skin and seeds. The resulting purée should have the consistency of light cream. If it is too thick, add as much of the vegetable stock as you need to thin it out. Season the soup with salt, pepper, chili oil and paprika.

Warm the milk in a small saucepan over low heat, whisking constantly. Add the Parmesan and whisk until the cheese has completely melted.

Remove the Parmesan cream from the heat and let it come to room temperature.

To serve, foam the Parmesan cream using a cappuccino steamer or hand blender. Pour the heated soup into cappuccino cups and top each serving with the foam, just as you would a cappuccino. Sprinkle a pinch of paprika over the Parmesan foam.

Fresh Tomato and Bread Soup

This is a renowned dish of Florence, served with pride at the finest dinners. Yet it's also a great favourite with children, and one of the first dishes anyone learns to make – because everybody has lots of two-day-old bread around. My father used to eat it cold with thinly sliced red onions. Pecorino or shaved Parmesan cheese is also a nice complement. And if you have some left over, serve it as a bread salad.

Ingredients

1 lb [500g]	ripe tomatoes
6 Tbsp [100 mL]	extra virgin olive oil
2 cloves	garlic, finely chopped
	small handful of basil, chopped
4	fresh sage leaves, chopped
1	small fresh chili pepper, finely chopped
	salt
	freshly ground black pepper
4 cups [1 L]	classic meat broth *(see page 159)* or chicken stock
2/3 lb [300 g]	2-day-old dense, crusty bread, firm but not dried out (about 1/2 loaf)
	extra virgin olive oil

Serves 6

Preparation

Remove tomato skins: cut a small *X* in the bottom of each tomato and dip the tomatoes into boiling water for 10 seconds. The skins will slide off easily. Coarsely chop the tomatoes.

In a large sauté pan, heat the olive oil over medium heat. Add the garlic and sauté until it turns blonde, then add tomatoes, basil, sage, chili, salt and pepper and cook uncovered 10 to 15 minutes, until the tomato is soft.

Meanwhile, bring the broth to a boil. When the tomato is cooked, add the hot broth and bring the mixture to a rapid boil. Turn off the heat.

Cut the bread into thin slices. Without removing the pan from the stove, put a layer of bread into the soup. It will absorb the liquid and sink to the bottom. Continue until all the bread is soaked. Cover the pan and allow it to rest for 10 minutes.

Serve the soup hot, warm or cold, with a drizzle of extra virgin olive oil.

TUSCAN MINESTRONE

What makes this minestrone Tuscan is that it includes cannellini beans and either cauliflower or cavolo nero, *a vegetable similar to kale. Yet every region of Tuscany has its own variation, depending on what grows there in abundance. In Florence they add spinach; in Grosseto, more onions. The Pisans like lots of beans and chickpeas. In Siena they like chickpeas too, and they also flavour it with sage and rosemary.*

INGREDIENTS

1 1/2 cups [375 mL]	dried cannellini (white kidney) beans
4 cups [1 L]	*cavolo nero* or kale, sliced
1/4	medium white cauliflower
2	medium zucchinis
2	medium leeks
1	medium onion
2	medium potatoes
2	medium carrots
2 stalks	celery, with leaves
2 cloves	garlic, finely chopped
2 Tbsp [30 mL]	tomato paste
1 tsp [5 mL]	Tuscan mixed spices or equal combination ground cloves, nutmeg, hot pepper flakes, coriander and curry
	salt
	freshly ground black pepper
	Parmesan cheese for garnish
	extra virgin olive oil

SERVES 6

PREPARATION

Soak the beans for 12 hours. Drain and rinse under cold running water. Place the beans in a large pot with 8 cups [2 L] lightly salted water and bring to a boil.

Reduce to a simmer and cook covered for 2 hours, or until beans are tender. *(See page 48 for more detailed instructions.)*

Remove half the beans and bean water and set aside. Pass the remaining beans and water through a food mill and return to large pot.

Cut the vegetables into equal-sized pieces. Add them with the garlic, tomato paste and spices to the creamed beans. Cook covered at a low boil for 30 minutes, stirring occasionally. Add the remaining beans and bean water and cook covered for a further 30 minutes. Add salt and pepper to taste.

Serve the soup hot with some grated Parmesan and a drizzle of extra virgin olive oil, or allow it to cool at room temperature before refrigerating, then serve it cold with the same garnishes.

TUSCAN CABBAGE AND BEAN SOUP

You can't separate Tuscan beans from Tuscan cabbage. They are staples that turn up almost every day. Here they are combined in my favourite soup. This soup goes by different names in the different regions of Tuscany, but always has the same ingredients and the same respect.

INGREDIENTS

1 head	savoy cabbage
1/4 cup [60 mL]	extra virgin olive oil
4	fresh, ripe tomatoes, coarsely chopped
6 cups [1.5 L]	water
1/2 cup [125 mL]	chopped zucchini
1 1/2 cups [375 mL]	cooked toscanelli or cannellini beans
1/2 cup [125 mL]	fresh peas
2	sage leaves
1 sprig	rosemary
1	bouquet garni of fresh mint, basil and dill salt
	freshly ground black pepper
6 thin slices	dense Tuscan bread
	Parmesan cheese

SERVES 6

PREPARATION

Separate the cabbage into leaves and wash and dry them.

Heat 2 Tbsp [30 mL] of the oil in a large pot over medium heat, and sauté the cabbage leaves for about 8 minutes, until they are soft but haven't browned. Add the tomatoes and cook for 5 more minutes.

Add the water, zucchini, beans, peas, sage, rosemary, bouquet garni and salt and pepper. Bring the soup to a boil, reduce the heat and simmer uncovered for about 40 minutes.

Place 2 slices of bread side by side on the bottom of a tureen, then pour on a good helping of the soup and drizzle on some of the remaining 2 Tbsp [30 mL] of olive oil. Repeat with 2 more slices of bread, more soup and more oil. Finish with the last of the bread, soup and olive oil.

Grate some Parmesan cheese on top, and it is ready to serve hot or cold.

TYRRHENIAN FISH SOUP

Zuppa di pesce is a dish you'll find all around the Italian coastline, from the Ligurian Sea to the Adriatic, with a variation approximately every four to five miles. Even along the Tuscan coastline you may find over a dozen variations. This one is most typical of the area from Forte dei Marmi to the island of Elba.

INGREDIENTS

4 Tbsp [60 mL]	extra virgin olive oil
1/2 cup [125 mL]	finely chopped onion
1/2 cup [125 mL]	finely chopped celery
2	cloves garlic, chopped
1 can	tomatoes (28 oz [796 mL])
20	black kalamata olives, pitted and coarsely chopped
4	anchovy fillets, washed and chopped
1 tsp [5 mL]	chopped fresh oregano
	freshly ground black pepper
1/4 cup [60 mL]	dry red wine
4	medium calamari, cleaned and cut into rings
8	prawns, peeled
12	clams in shell
12	mussels in shell
1/2 lb [250 g]	red snapper, cut in 4 pieces
4 slices	dense Tuscan bread
2 cloves	garlic, cut in half

SERVES 4

PREPARATION

Heat the olive oil in a large saucepan over medium heat. Sauté the onions and celery until they turn transparent, then add the garlic. Continue sautéing for about 1 minute, or until the onions and celery pick up a bit of brown. Add the tomatoes, olives, anchovies, oregano and pepper. Break up the tomatoes with a wooden spoon. Simmer uncovered for 20 minutes.

Add the red wine and simmer another 10 minutes. Add the calamari, prawns, clams, mussels and red snapper all together. Simmer until the clams and mussels open up, approximately 10 minutes. Taste and see if salt is necessary, and add more black pepper if you like.

Grill or toast a slice of Tuscan bread per person. Rub each slice with half a clove of garlic. Put a slice in each bowl. Take a big tureen of soup to the table and spoon the soup over the bread.

Salads in Tuscany are an example of
       meno è meglio, less is more. A slice of mature tomato with olive oil is
so complex it confuses the mind into thinking there must be more.

Salads

GRILLED BEEF WITH ARUGULA AND SHAVED PARMESAN

I can't think of anything as tasty and clean as this steak salad. It is simple to prepare, but you have to wait for it. The beef must marinate in the herbs and oil for at least two hours to absorb their subtle flavours. This is a dish to linger over on a sunny afternoon. Add a plate of pommes frites and you have perfection. A lot of people are in too much of a hurry to spend this much time on their food – and I guess they'll just have to miss out on the rewards.

INGREDIENTS

one 2 lb [1 kg]	well-aged sirloin steak, 2 in. [5 cm] thick
1 Tbsp [15 mL]	extra virgin olive oil
2 cloves	garlic
2 sprigs	rosemary
2 sprigs	sage
	handful of arugula
2 Tbsp [30 mL]	extra virgin olive oil
	juice of 1 lemon
	salt
	freshly ground black pepper
4–5 shavings	fresh Parmesan cheese per person

SERVES 4 AS A MAIN COURSE,
8 AS AN APPETIZER

PREPARATION

Rub the meat on both sides with the 1 Tbsp [15 mL] of oil. Mince together the garlic, rosemary and sage, and spread on both sides of the beef. Refrigerate the meat for at least 2 hours.

Heat the barbecue as hot as it will go. Scrape the steak clean of the herb mixture. Place the steak on the grill and leave it alone until one side is cooked, 8 to 10 minutes. Turn it and grill for another 5 to 8 minutes, or until it has reached your preferred level of doneness.

Remove the steak to a warmed platter.

Cover it and let it rest for 10 minutes. Cut the steak into 1/4 in. [5 mm] slices, cutting on a 45 degree angle from top to bottom. Divide the slices among individual plates. (The meat will be lukewarm when you serve it.)

Toss the arugula with the 2 Tbsp [30 mL] oil. Add the lemon juice and salt and pepper and toss again. Divide the arugula among the plates, arranging it on top of the beef.

Use a vegetable peeler to shave the Parmesan over the arugula – 4 or 5 shavings per person.

RECOMMENDED WINE
Carmignano Riserva
RECOMMENDED PRODUCERS
Fattoria Ambra, Bacchereto, Tenuta di Capezzana, Le Farnete, Iolanda Pratesi, Villa di Trefiano
There is 10 to 15 per cent Cabernet in Carmignano, which pairs it nicely with the rich grilled flavours of the beef and the highly aromatic Parmesan.

GREEN BEAN, TUNA AND POTATO SALAD

Canned tuna is affordable and available everywhere, and Tuscans love to use it creatively. This is a beloved dish in summer, not just as a salad but also as an hors d'oeuvre. It works equally well with white beans.

INGREDIENTS

2	large potatoes, preferably Yukon Gold, skins on
2	eggs
1/2 lb [250 g]	green beans, strings removed OR 1 1/4 cups [300 mL] cooked cannellini beans
1 Tbsp [15 mL]	olive oil
	juice of 1 lemon
	salt
	freshly ground black pepper
1 can	oil-packed flaked tuna, with oil (6 1/2 oz [184 g])
1	medium onion, coarsely chopped
2 Tbsp [25 mL]	capers
1 sprig	parsley, chopped
1 clove	garlic, finely chopped
1/4 cup [50 mL]	mayonnaise
	dash of Tabasco

SERVES 4

PREPARATION

Boil the potatoes whole in salted water. When they are tender, drain them and remove the skins. Cool the potatoes before slicing. Cut them in half lengthwise then slice in half-rounds and set aside.

Hard-cook the eggs: place them in cold water and bring to a boil. Immediately turn off the heat and leave the eggs in the water for at least 10 minutes.

Boil the beans in salted water until they are tender but still firm to the bite. Drain them well.

Toss the beans in a large bowl with the oil, lemon juice and salt and pepper. Add the sliced potatoes and the tuna with its oil, and mix very gently. Taste for seasonings and add more salt and pepper, if necessary. Add the onion, capers, parsley, garlic, mayonnaise and Tabasco and mix very gently.

To serve, divide the salad among individual plates and garnish with quarters of hard-cooked egg.

MUSHROOM SEASON

Tuscany claims to have the largest selection of mushrooms anywhere. We could talk about these wonderful fungi forever and ever (maybe in my next cookbook), but for now I want to share the basic Tuscan approach.

MUSHROOM SEASON is a total regional commitment. In school, kids learn to identify the different varieties of *funghi*, and in the newspaper the local commune publishes pictures and descriptions. With all those people out looking and all those kinds of mushrooms growing, so many of them poisonous, proper identification is crucial. It's so easy to make a fatal mistake.

When the season draws near in late August, tension starts to build as the men and women of Tuscany anxiously prepare themselves for the physical and mental exertions to come. We are talking about territorial mushroom wars, where strangers are looked on with suspicion as regions protect the mushroom grounds from outside invaders. We are talking about solo trips into the woods for days, hiding your own footsteps so nobody can discover your secret spot, not even the closest members of your family.

I remember Mother suspecting my father of having an affair because he could not explain where he had been all one day, especially because he had returned home without a single mushroom. But he couldn't reveal his secret place, even to save himself.

A mushroom hunter must be wary. Spies are everywhere, listening in on conversations, following cars down lonely roads, watching mushroom pickers with binoculars from upper stories of houses – everyone wants to sink their teeth and noses into that first pick of wild porcini or *cantarelli* (chanterelles).

Finally the moment comes when a sack is opened on the kitchen counter to reveal its earth-speckled nuggets. In the market, tomatoes and onions are moved from the centre of the vegetable displays to make room for baskets of just-picked mushrooms. Lineups appear outside the restaurants that are known to have a way with *funghi*.

We have a local expression that we use when someone's distracted or not paying attention: *Funghi in testa?* Have you got mushrooms on the brain? Come mushroom season in Tuscany, everybody acts as if they have *funghi in testa*.

PORCINI EXTRA
2500
L etto

MUSHROOMS WITH A BITE

A favourite Tuscan joke is about two widows sharing their life stories.

"Lucia," says Rosa, "Five times you've been married and five times you've been widowed. What terrible tragedies took your five husbands away from you?"

"My first, Mario, ate some poisonous mushrooms," says Lucia, "and my second, Giuliano, died from poisonous mushrooms too."

"What a terrible coincidence. What happened to your third?" asks Rosa.

"Ah, Emilio," says Lucia. "He had the misfortune to eat poisonous mushrooms also."

"You certainly had a fondness for mushroom pickers," says Rosa. "What happened to number four?"

"Oh, dear Stefano. It was his stomach. He lingered for days in terrible pain."

"Cancer?"

"Mushrooms."

"Lucia, what awful luck you have," says Rosa. "And how did you lose your last dear husband?" Lucia sighs and shakes her head. "I had to hit him over the head with the pan because he wouldn't eat the mushrooms."

SUMMER TOMATO SALAD

In summertime the tomato is king and it's rare not to find this salad on the table. It would be a sin to ignore tomatoes and cucumbers at the peak of their glory.

INGREDIENTS

4	large, firm tomatoes
2	young long cucumbers

PARSLEY-MINT DRESSING

	juice of 1 lemon
1 Tbsp [15 mL]	white wine vinegar
	salt
1 sprig	parsley, chopped
1 sprig	fresh mint, chopped
	crushed black pepper
4 Tbsp [65 mL]	extra virgin olive oil

SERVES 4 TO 6

PREPARATION

Slice the tomatoes fairly thin and arrange them in 2 rows on a platter. Peel the cucumber, thinly slice it and arrange the slices alongside the tomatoes.

In a small bowl, combine the lemon juice, vinegar, salt, parsley, mint and pepper. Whisk them quickly until the surface becomes foamy. Gradually add the oil and whisk until it reaches a creamy consistency.

Pour the dressing over the tomatoes and cucumber, cover the platter and chill in the fridge for 1 hour. Just before serving, add more pepper and salt to taste.

TOMATO AND BOCCONCINI SALAD FOR TWO

The best bocconcini, or fresh mozzarella, is made from the milk of water buffaloes. This salad can also be made with cow's milk mozzarella, if buffalo mozzarella isn't available.

INGREDIENTS

4 Tbsp [65 mL]	balsamic vinegar
1/2 tsp [2 mL]	sugar
2	medium roma tomatoes
	salt
	freshly ground black pepper
	pinch of sugar
1 ball	bocconcini (about 2 oz [50 g]), sliced
6–10	medium basil leaves, finely chopped
2 Tbsp [30 mL]	extra virgin olive oil

SERVES 2

PREPARATION

Make a reduction of balsamic vinegar by simmering the vinegar and sugar in a small pot over medium heat. Stir frequently, until the liquid is reduced to about 1/4 of its original volume. Set aside.

Slice each tomato in 4 and overlap the slices in circles on 2 plates. Season with salt and pepper, as well as a pinch of sugar if the tomatoes aren't flavourful enough. Arrange the bocconcini slices on the tomatoes. Garnish with the chopped basil.

Drizzle the balsamic reduction around the plate and the olive oil on top of the mozzarella.

A TOUCH OF GREEN

In Tuscany, the wind carries the perfume of herbs, which grow like weeds in the fields and forests, and the kitchen is filled with the aromas of those herbs as they flavour whatever is cooking in the wood-burning oven. In each region, a different combination of wood and herbs flavours bread and roasting meat, depending on what grows best there.

IN THE PINE, CHESTNUT or oak forests of Tuscany, *boscaioli*, loggers, cut down older and damaged trees to give the forest a healthier and longer life. It is an ecological relationship that has been going on for centuries. More light filters through the foliage and warms up the moist soil, encouraging mushrooms and herbs to grow. The wood goes to the farmers, who warm their large homes and use the same fire for cooking the mushrooms and herbs they have harvested from the forest.

Herbs are essential to Tuscan cooking. We pick aromatics like sage, rosemary and wild fennel, and we grow them in every garden and on every apartment balcony. We also look out for *ortica*, or nettles, to use in pasta dishes, and chamomile to boil for tea, among other wild greens. There's definitely no shortage.

I have noticed a revival of interest in herbs among people who have abandoned their family farms and moved to the industrialized areas to make a better living. Now they are returning, wanting to rediscover nature and recapture the taste of the wild herbs they ate and collected as children.

When I was growing up on a farm near Florence, my weekly duty was to pick wild chicory along the roadside. I would pick it on my way home from school, especially after the rain when it was nice and green. Mamma boiled it in a pot of rainwater with a bit of salt, then tossed it with fresh oil and pecorino cheese. My efforts earned me an afternoon away from doing my painstaking homework, even though I didn't eat the chicory.

At Villa Delia, I take my students on long walks to find these sometimes-forgotten delicacies and to share with them the stories of the area. Many times we run into locals out on a stroll. They see a group of us picking herbs and I can hear them saying *Che bravi questi stranieri*, What nice people these foreigners are. Or they greet us with *Una bella giornata*. The literal translation, a beautiful day, in no way conveys the depth of sincerity behind this phrase.

A beautiful day comes about because you've taken the step of going out. On a beautiful day, you meet a friend unexpectedly. You enjoy the sight of the priest playing soccer with some kids, or watch a pussycat stretched out in the sun on top of a stone fence, so lazy that it lets a flock of birds walk by. The herbs you take home are served with love as a salad, in a frittata or subtly scenting a roast chicken. Going out the door is a small effort that brings many rewards.

HANDLING FRESH HERBS

A sprig of herb is the amount you can pick with three fingers. With three fingers you will get the newest growth, without a lot of woody stem.

Think of fresh herbs as aroma, not spice. Go for delicate flavour rather than pungency. You don't need to use a lot. If you're cooking with liquid, delicate herbs such as basil and dill should either be cooked very gently or added at the end of cooking, to prevent their flavour from disappearing.

Delicate herbs should ideally be ripped instead of cut with a knife (parsley is an exception). Contact with a knife can make them bitter, and most of the aromatic oils will end up on the chopping board.

If you have to buy herbs, buy just what you need. Herbs lose about 70 per cent of their flavour if they're refrigerated. Better yet, you might consider growing them for a reliable supply. They're easy to grow and don't take up much room, even on an apartment balcony.

SEASIDE RICE SALAD

This is a great summer salad and a nice addition to a buffet.

INGREDIENTS

1 cup [250 mL]	Arborio rice
	salt
1/2 cup [125 mL]	shrimp
1/2 cup [125 mL]	calamari, cleaned
6–8	mussels, in the shell
1/4 cup [50 mL]	dry white wine
	juice of 1/2 lemon
1/2 cup [125 mL]	water
1 sprig	parsley
1 clove	garlic, whole
	freshly ground black pepper
1/4 cup [50 mL]	extra virgin olive oil
2 cloves	garlic, whole
1/2 cup [125 mL]	diced fresh tomatoes
1 stalk	parsley, chopped
	radicchio leaves for garnish
	juice of 1/2 lemon

SERVES 4

RECOMMENDED WINE
Elba Bianco

RECOMMENDED PRODUCERS
Acquabona, Tenuta la Chiusa
Pliny the Elder spoke of Elba wines as being sturdy. One suspects Etruscan wines were very different from this light, fruity, modern-day Elba white, which is seemingly tailor-made for this delicious salad.

PREPARATION

Put the rice in 4 cups [1 L] salted water and bring it to a boil. Keep it at a low boil, uncovered, for 15 to 20 minutes, or until al dente. When the rice is cooked, drain it and rinse with cold water. Drain the rice again, place it in a bowl and set it aside to come to room temperature.

Shell and devein the shrimp if necessary. Bring a large pot of salted water to a boil. Put the shrimp in the water and remove them with a slotted spoon as soon as they turn pink, 20 seconds to 2 minutes depending on the size of the shrimp. Place them in a bowl and set aside.

Return the water to a boil and blanch the calamari. Plunge the calamari into the water and remove them the moment they turn opaque (almost instantaneously). Dice the calamari and set aside.

Remove any seaweed or grit from the mussels. Combine the wine, lemon juice, water, parsley, 1 garlic clove, salt and pepper in a small pot. Add the mussels and bring to a boil. Remove the mussels when they open.

Heat 2 Tbsp [25 mL] of the oil in a pan large enough to contain all the ingredients. Sauté the 2 garlic cloves until they are golden, then discard. Quickly toss the shrimp, calamari, mussels and diced tomatoes together in the hot oil, then remove from the heat. Allow the mixture to come to room temperature.

To prepare the salad, toss the seafood mixture with the rice and chopped parsley. Cover and refrigerate for at least an hour before serving.

To serve, place some rice salad on a few leaves of radicchio, drizzle the remaining oil around it and squeeze on some lemon juice.

VEGETABLE AND FRUIT SALAD

Gorgonzola and truffle oil in the dressing add rich overtones to this sophisticated salad.

INGREDIENTS

2	eggs
1/2 lb [250 g]	tiny green beans
2	small beets
1	small field cucumber
4	shallots
1	firm pear
1	green apple
1	fresh red chili
1 small head	leaf lettuce, separated into leaves
1/4 cup [50 mL]	shelled walnuts
1 sprig	mint, chopped
1 sprig	chervil, chopped
1 sprig	basil, chopped
1 sprig	Italian flat-leafed parsley, chopped

ORANGE-GORGONZOLA DRESSING

3 cloves	garlic
	point end of 1 red chili
	pinch of coarse salt
	freshly ground black pepper
6 Tbsp [90 mL]	truffle-infused olive oil
3 Tbsp [45 mL]	apple cider vinegar
4 oz [125 g]	Gorgonzola cheese
2 Tbsp [25 mL]	plain yogurt
1 Tbsp [15 mL]	fresh orange juice

SERVES 6 TO 8

PREPARATION

Hard-cook the eggs, starting them in cold water, bringing the water to a boil and turning off the heat. Let them sit covered for 10 minutes.

Blanch the beans in a pot of boiling salted water for 3 to 4 minutes, until they are bright green and pleasantly tender. Plunge them in cold water to prevent further cooking. Once they are cool, drain the beans well.

Bring another pot of salted water to boil. Peel and dice the beets. Drop them into boiling salted water and boil covered for 10 minutes, or until they are firm but tender. Drain them well.

Peel the cucumber and cut the flesh away from the seed core in long strips. Cut the strips crosswise into matchsticks. Peel and finely slice the shallots. Peel, core and slice the pear and the apple. Cut the eggs into quarters. Scrape the seeds and ribs out of the chili and finely dice it.

Arrange the lettuce leaves on a flat platter and pile the ingredients on top, one layer at a time: beans, beets, cucumber, shallots, pear, apple, eggs, finely diced chili, walnuts and chopped herbs.

To make the dressing, put all ingredients in a mortar or food processor and blend to a creamy liquid. If it is too dense, add a bit of warm water.

Pour the dressing over the salad and gently toss everything together so the ingredients are coated but still in layers. Finish with a dusting of freshly ground black pepper if desired.

Lentil Salad with Watercress and Lettuce

Lentils are a healthy staple at any time of the year, and they make a nice starch variation in the summer. I can't say lentils are one of my favourite foods, but if I'm going to eat them, I like to call on the help of my friend watercress.

Ingredients

4 cups [1 L]	water
1 1/2 cups [375 mL]	lentils, rinsed
1	bay leaf
	pinch of salt
	freshly ground black pepper
3/4 cup [175 mL]	extra virgin olive oil
1/4 cup [50 mL]	red wine vinegar
1	red bell pepper, diced
1	yellow bell pepper, diced
4	green onions, sliced
2 cloves	garlic, minced
4	sundried tomatoes, cut in slivers
1 bunch	watercress, washed, stemmed and dried
1 small head	butter lettuce, washed, torn and dried
1–2	fresh tomatoes, cut in wedges

Serves 4

Preparation

Bring water to a boil and add the lentils, bay leaf, salt and pepper. Reduce heat to medium-low and simmer the lentils covered for 45 minutes. Drain if necessary and discard the bay leaf.

Make a vinaigrette by whisking together the olive oil and vinegar. Toss the hot lentils in 1/2 of the mixture.

Add the peppers, green onions, garlic and sundried tomatoes to the lentils. Refrigerate the salad if you will be serving it cold.

Just before serving, toss the watercress and lettuce with the remaining vinaigrette and arrange on a serving platter. Serve the lentils warm or cold atop the greens. Garnish with tomato wedges.

RADICCHIO, BEET AND APPLE SALAD

Here is a good light and healthy lunch – especially when it's served under a pergola in the summer, and married with a glass of white wine. For even greater health benefits, make it a three-hour lunch. Salute!

INGREDIENTS

2	large beets
2	green apples
1 head	radicchio, julienned
1 head	curly endive, pulled apart
1/4 cup [60 mL]	liquid from boiling beets
1 tsp [5 mL]	cornstarch

APPLE CIDER DRESSING

2 Tbsp [25 mL]	apple cider vinegar
2 Tbsp [25 mL]	apple juice
6 Tbsp [85 mL]	olive oil
	salt
	freshly ground black pepper

SERVES 4

PREPARATION

Wash and peel the beets, then boil them until tender. Remove the beets from the liquid, retaining 1/4 cup [60 mL] of the liquid. Cool the beets, slice them into 1/4 in. [5 mm] thick rounds and quarter the rounds.

Peel and core the apple, and cut it into 1/4 in. [5 mm] slices.

Pour the beet liquid into a small pot over medium heat. Stir in the cornstarch in until it dissolves completely. Heat the juice, stirring, until the juice thickens. Allow it to cool before serving.

In a large bowl, whisk together the vinegar, apple juice, olive oil and salt and pepper to make a dressing. Toss the beets, apples, radicchio and curly endive with the dressing.

To serve, divide the salad among 4 plates and drizzle the thickened beet juice around the plate to create a colourful accent.

ORANGE AND FENNEL SALAD

Pomegranate molasses is a thick, dark syrup that is rich and tart at the same time. It is available at Middle Eastern specialty shops. You can substitute balsamic vinegar that has been reduced by two-thirds and is thick and syrupy.

INGREDIENTS

4	oranges, peeled and sliced crosswise
1 bulb	fennel, finely shaved
2	pears, peeled, cored and cut in small wedges
1 head	curly endive, torn into bite-sized pieces
	salt
1 tsp [5mL]	fennel seeds, toasted and crushed

POMEGRANATE MOLASSES DRESSING

2 Tbsp [25 mL]	pomegranate molasses or reduced balsamic vinegar
4 Tbsp [60 mL]	extra virgin olive oil
	pinch of salt
4	water crackers or toast points for garnish

SERVES 4

PREPARATION

Gently mix the orange slices, fennel, pears and endive in a bowl. Sprinkle with a bit of salt and the toasted, crushed fennel seeds.

In another small bowl, whisk the pomegranate molasses or reduced balsamic vinegar with the olive oil and a pinch of salt. Pour the dressing over the salad and gently toss everything together.

Mound the salad on 4 plates and garnish with crackers. The pomegranate molasses and olive oil will separate slightly, creating a beautiful broken sauce of rich mahogany and olive green.

RED CABBAGE SALAD

The attic is the Tuscan equivalent of the North American root cellar. In the days before houses were insulated, the cellar stayed cold enough to store food, but warm enough not to freeze, because of the warmth rising from the house. The attic was also nice and dry because of the north-facing window which admitted the dry northern winds. For a salad like this, someone would collect the cabbage, carrots and onions from the attic and find some hardy winter greens in the garden.

INGREDIENTS

1/8 tsp [0.5 mL]	salt
1/4 tsp [1 mL]	freshly ground black pepper
2 Tbsp [25 mL]	apple cider vinegar
1/4 cup [50 mL]	extra virgin olive oil
1 bunch	curly endive, washed and torn into bite-sized pieces
1/8	medium red cabbage, very finely sliced
2	medium carrots, grated
4	green onions, sliced
	alfalfa, mixed bean or sunflower sprouts for garnish

SERVES 4

PREPARATION

Put the salt and pepper into a small, deep bowl and whisk in the vinegar. When the vinegar gets foamy it has opened up and is ready to receive the oil. Add the oil slowly, whisking it quickly to mix well.

Toss the endive, cabbage, carrots and green onions with the vinaigrette in a salad bowl. Adjust the seasonings to taste.

Refrigerate the salad for 1 hour or so to mingle the flavours before serving. Garnish with sprouts.

VEGETABLES

*We have always eaten with the seasons so we
get the freshest and most intensely flavoured food.
Over the centuries we've learned
how to prepare foods to get the most flavour out of them.*

ARTICHOKES IN A POT

These tender artichokes are traditionally served with young lamb or as part of an antipasto platter. They're delicious warm or cold. When you're buying fresh artichokes, get them as fresh and plump as possible. Any wrinkles on the leaves or stem mean they've started to dry out.

INGREDIENTS

1	lemon
10	small fresh artichokes
4 Tbsp [60 mL]	extra virgin olive oil
	handful of parsley
4 cloves	garlic, chopped
1 cup [250 mL]	classic meat broth *(see page 159)* or chicken stock
	salt
	freshly ground black pepper

SERVES 6 TO 8

PREPARATION

Squeeze the juice of 1/2 the lemon into a large bowl of cold water. As you expose new surfaces of the artichokes, dip them into this acidulated water to prevent discoloration. Remove the tough outer leaves of the artichokes and cut 1/2 in. [1 cm] off the tops off all the remaining leaves. Trim the stems. Cut each artichoke in half vertically and remove the fuzzy choke. Cut in half again. Swirl the quarters in the acidulated water to wash them. Drain.

Pour the oil into a pot large enough to hold all the artichokes standing up. Arrange the artichokes, add the parsley and garlic and squeeze in the juice of the other 1/2 lemon. Pour in the broth and add salt and pepper. Cook uncovered over low heat for 30 to 40 minutes, or until you can easily remove an outer leaf.

Turn off the heat, cover the pot and let the artichokes sweat for 20 to 30 minutes. This rest will help them pick up all the other flavours. Serve warm or cold.

GILDED CARROTS

These carrots are very creamy and cheesy. They go well with roast pork, turkey or beef and with lamb chops.

INGREDIENTS

1 lb [500 g]	medium carrots
3 Tbsp [45 mL]	butter
1 Tbsp [15 mL]	extra virgin olive oil
	salt
2	eggs
1/4 cup [50 mL]	whipping cream
1/4 lb [125 g]	freshly grated Parmesan cheese
2 sprigs	fresh mint, chopped
1 sprig	parsley, chopped
1 Tbsp [15 mL]	dry sherry

SERVES 4 TO 6

PREPARATION

Preheat the oven to 400°F [200°C].

Peel the carrots and cook them whole in boiling water for about 5 minutes. They will still be very firm. Cut them into 1/4 in. [5 mm] slices. Heat the butter and oil in a skillet over medium heat. Add the carrots, sprinkle them with salt and sauté for about a minute.

Transfer the carrots to an ovenproof dish. In a bowl, beat the eggs with the cream, Parmesan, herbs and sherry. Spread the mixture over the carrots. Bake them for about 20 minutes or until golden, and serve.

Beans

For a long time beans were kind of a Tuscan family secret. At home, not a week went by – often not a day – when beans didn't appear on the table. But it would be shameful to serve them to someone because "Oh, it's the only food we have – it's poor man's food. How can we give it to a guest?" The secret got out though, and to the rest of Italy we are known as mangiafagioli: *bean-eaters.*

SUDDENLY WE'RE BEING TOLD that beans are a superfood: they've got fibre, phytochemicals, B vitamins, minerals, protein.... Now people from the cities head to the country in search of the best-prepared bean soup or best-cooked beans. Our humble staple is in style.

Of course our cultural attachment to beans has nothing to do with fashion. If anything, we're against innovation. But we're not against variety. I take my cooking school guests from restaurant to restaurant, and everybody serves beans, but each dish is different.

Close to the coast you see more combinations with seafood. Near the agricultural centres you'll find hearty beans and sausage or game or pork. The seasons also determine what we do with them. In summertime you see beans only in salad. In winter they'll be in soups, to keep us warm. These things do not change.

Tuscans generally use white beans, either the white kidney beans called cannellini or the smaller white beans called navy beans in English. For a short time in May the beans are green and tender and we steam them in garlic and oil and lemon. Then for a few weeks they are halfway to being dry and they're boiled and drizzled with olive oil and served as a garnish for white meat. A few weeks more and they are dried, to sustain our bodies – and souls – for the rest of the year.

In Tuscany, from the time you're four or five years old you know how to boil dried beans. Here is the way my grandmother taught me. I can't be exact about time or heat or salt because I don't know your pot or stove or palate, but I can give you the self-confidence to cook them to please your own mouth – tender or al dente, suit yourself.

Soften the beans overnight in cold water. Our beans are grown locally and cleaned by hand, so soaking washes off any dust and impurities. It also tenderizes the skins.

Remove the beans from the soaking water and put them into a pot of salted water – very big pot, lots of water so the beans have room to move around and they won't become sticky. Tuscans often collect rainwater or water from streams in the hills to cook them in because the softer water makes them taste better.

Add a rosemary branch and 4 whole cloves of garlic along with the soaked beans. Cover the pot and bring the water to a boil. Lower the heat and keep the beans at a gentle boil, covered, for about an hour. When they are soft and pleasant to the bite, they're done. Only a few of them should have split skins. If they're all split and exploded you've boiled them too hard. Overcooked beans will be pasty and won't absorb flavours anymore, so they won't work in combination with other foods.

Put the beans in a strainer and drain them. If you're using them immediately they won't need rinsing – unless you cooked them in not enough water! If you want to use the beans later, rinse them in cold water to stop the cooking. Toss them with a little olive oil and keep them in the fridge. Later, if you want to warm them up, just dip them in a pot of hot water. I always make beans in big batches so I will have some to use when I need them.

Tuscans don't fool around with beans; we say it's sacrilegious. As you'll see in the recipes throughout the book, we like to just let them be and let nature take control.

Green Beans with Garlic

Green beans appear almost all year round on the Italian table. In Tuscany they are as important as asparagus or zucchini, all of them friendly vegetables that go with any kind of meat. This recipe works for all of them if you adjust the cooking times. I like these beans with meat or on their own as a salad or an hors d'oeuvre.

Ingredients

2 Tbsp [30 mL]	extra virgin olive oil
1	medium onion, diced
2 cloves	garlic, chopped
1 cup [250 mL]	chopped fresh tomatoes
1 Tbsp [15 mL]	tomato paste
1/2 tsp [2 mL]	sugar
	salt
	freshly ground black pepper
1/2 cup [125 mL]	water
1 lb [500 g]	fresh green beans, strings removed
2 tsp [10 mL]	chopped parsley
	walnut oil for garnish

Serves 6

Preparation

Heat the olive oil over medium heat and sauté the onion until it's transparent. Add the garlic and toss it with the onion for a few seconds, then add tomatoes, tomato paste, sugar, salt and pepper and water. Cover and simmer for 10 minutes.

Add the beans and parsley, replace the lid and cook for about 20 minutes, or until the beans are tender.

Serve the beans hot or cold, and finish with a drizzle of walnut oil.

Porri brasati

BRAISED LEEKS

This is a great vegetable side dish that also works as an antipasto dish. It can be served warm or chilled.

INGREDIENTS

6	medium leeks
2 Tbsp [25 mL]	olive oil
1	medium onion, sliced
2 Tbsp [25 mL]	tomato paste
1/2 cup [125 mL]	water
2 Tbsp [25 mL]	chopped parsley
1 tsp [5 mL]	brown sugar
	salt
	freshly ground black pepper
	juice of 1/2 lemon
1 tsp [5 mL]	chopped fresh dill for garnish
	lemon slices for garnish

SERVES 4 TO 6

PREPARATION

Remove any tough outer leaves from the leeks, trim off the roots and cut off the darker green tops, leaving only the white and light green parts. Cut the leeks in half lengthwise and wash them well to remove any sand.

Heat the oil in a skillet over medium heat and sauté the onion until soft. Add the tomato paste, water, parsley, sugar, salt and pepper and mix well. Bring the liquid to a boil, then reduce the heat, cover the pan and simmer the sauce for 10 minutes.

Add the leeks and lemon juice, cover and simmer 15 to 20 minutes more, or until the leeks are tender. Transfer to a serving dish and garnish with dill and lemon slices.

SAUTÉED FENNEL WITH ROSEMARY AND ORANGE

These two flavours are traditionally associated with winter. Fennel is at its sweetest from fall through spring. And oranges are the fruit of celebration in Tuscany. I would always get oranges and mandarins along with a few chocolates in my Christmas stocking. Serve this as a starter or a side dish with meat or grilled fish. Try it with your turkey for a Tuscan-flavoured Christmas dinner.

INGREDIENTS

4 medium bulbs	fennel
	vegetable oil
	salt
	freshly ground black pepper
1 small sprig	rosemary
4	oranges, preferably blood oranges
	coarse sea salt
	extra virgin olive oil
1 tsp [5 mL]	chopped mint leaves

SERVES 4

PREPARATION

Discard the tough outer skin and stem of the fennel bulbs. Wash the bulbs under cold water and slice crosswise into rounds 1/4 in. [5 mm] thick.

Over medium heat, place a large sauté pan with a heavy, thick bottom. Add just enough vegetable oil to coat the bottom, then add the fennel. Season with salt and pepper and lay the rosemary across the top.

Gently brown the fennel for 10 minutes on each side. Some pieces will come apart in the pan and this is fine. The fennel should be al dente.

With a spatula, transfer the fennel to a serving platter and keep it warm. Season again with salt and pepper. Remove the skin and pith from the oranges and slice the fruit 1/4 in. [5 mm] thick. Place orange slices on top of the fennel and season with coarse salt. Drizzle extra virgin olive oil over both the oranges and fennel and sprinkle with mint.

Serve warm. The warmth of the caramelized fennel will soften the oranges.

MASHED POTATOES BAKED WITH EGGS AND CHEESE

These mashed potatoes develop a nice crispy crust on the bottom. Make sure everybody gets some of it when you serve them.

INGREDIENTS

4	medium baking potatoes, skins on
6 Tbsp [80 mL]	butter
2	eggs
1 cup [250 mL]	freshly grated Parmesan cheese
1 cup [250 mL]	milk
	salt
	freshly ground black pepper

SERVES 4 TO 6

PREPARATION

Boil the potatoes until tender. Drain and peel them while they're still hot.

Preheat the oven to 400°F [200°C]. Grease a baking dish with the butter.

In a bowl, mash the potatoes. Add the eggs, Parmesan, milk, salt and pepper, mixing thoroughly. Transfer the mixture to the greased baking dish and bake for about 30 minutes, or until the potatoes get some colour on top.

STUFFED ROASTED BELL PEPPERS

In Tuscany, you'll see peppers only at the height of summer when they are in the garden, and you'll usually see them either grilled or stuffed. These stuffed peppers can be served one per person as a main dish, or one-half per person as part of an antipasto platter. You can also cut them into wedges and serve them cold alongside a rice salad.

INGREDIENTS

8	bell peppers, any colour
2 Tbsp [25 mL]	olive oil
2	medium onions, finely chopped
4 cloves	garlic, chopped
1/4 lb [125 g]	raw skinless chicken breast, diced
8 sprigs	parsley, chopped
5 oz [150 g]	spicy Italian sausage, removed from casing
2 oz [60 g]	dry salami, diced
2 slices	2-day-old bread
1 cup [250 mL]	milk
1 tsp [5 mL]	freshly grated nutmeg
	freshly ground black pepper
1/2 cup [125 mL]	freshly grated Parmesan cheese
2	eggs, beaten
	extra virgin olive oil

SERVES 8

PREPARATION

Cut off the tops of all the peppers and remove the seeds and ribs without splitting the flesh. Wash the peppers inside and out. Stand them up, tightly packed, in an ovenproof pan large enough to hold them all.

Heat the oil in a medium skillet and sauté the onions over medium-low heat until they are golden brown. Add the garlic and cook for another 1 or 2 minutes.

Add the chicken, parsley, sausage meat and salami. Mix well and cook another 5 to 8 minutes.

Soak the bread in the milk until it has absorbed all it can, then squeeze out the milk. Break the moistened bread into pieces and add them to the meat mixture. Stir in the nutmeg and black pepper and mix well. Remove from the heat.

Add the Parmesan and the eggs to the meat mixture and combine well. Cool the mixture to room temperature.

Preheat the oven to 375°F [190°C].

Stuff the peppers with the filling and drizzle with a little extra virgin olive oil. Roast in the oven for 30 minutes, then reduce the heat to 350°F [180°C] and roast for a further 15 minutes. The peppers will be browned a bit.

Serve hot or cold.

STUFFED ZUCCHINI, MY MOTHER'S STYLE

My sisters and brother and I celebrated the arrival of zucchinis on the table for two reasons. First, we loved the way our mother cooked them. Second, when zucchinis appeared, summer wasn't far behind, and with it, the end of school. Serve these with a salad of mixed greens for a great vegetarian meal.

INGREDIENTS

6	medium zucchinis, left whole
2 Tbsp [30 mL]	extra virgin olive oil
1/2	red onion, finely chopped
6 cloves	garlic, minced
	salt
	freshly ground black pepper
	dash of cayenne pepper
3	eggs
1/2 cup [125 mL]	freshly grated Parmesan cheese
1/2 tsp [2 mL]	grated nutmeg
2 Tbsp [30 mL]	chopped fresh parsley

SERVES 6 AS A MAIN COURSE,
12 AS A SIDE VEGETABLE

PREPARATION

Blanch the zucchinis for approximately 6 minutes in a large pot of boiling water then remove from the water and cut in half lengthwise. Scoop out the middle of each zucchini, creating a trough in the centre. Leave enough pulp around the edges so they won't collapse as they cook.

In a sauté pan, heat the olive oil and add the onion, garlic and scooped-out zucchini centres, as well as salt, pepper and cayenne to taste. Cook for approximately 4 to 5 minutes, or until the mixture is cooked and soft.

Preheat the oven to 350°F [180°C].

Remove the mixture from the sauté pan and put into the food processor. Add the eggs, Parmesan, nutmeg and parsley to the food processor as well, and process to a moist consistency and a mousselike texture.

Fill each hollowed-out zucchini with the processed mixture and place in a baking dish. Bake in the oven for 20 to 30 minutes.

Remove from the oven and place zucchinis on a serving platter as a garnish or, for a summer lunch, serve two half zucchinis as a main course.

EXTRA VIRGIN OLIVE OIL

If you find yourself staring at a shelf of olive oils trying to decide which to buy, you're not alone. The colours range from pale golden to brilliant green, and a tiny wax-sealed flask costs more than a two-litre bottle – yet they're all labelled extra virgin. With so many brands, places of origin and levels of quality, olive oil can be a complicated subject even for the experts.

DESPITE ALL THE PUBLICITY that olive oil receives these days, I think it still isn't understood very well. I would like to give you a basic understanding of this liquid gold that is so much a part of this book and of Italian cooking.

I call it liquid gold because good extra virgin olive oil is expensive. As a producer, I know that in a lucky year I might manage to produce 1 1/2 litres of oil per tree. You can imagine how many trees it takes to produce enough oil to make a living. Good oil is scarce, and worldwide demand drives the price up. As a consumer, though, I'll pay what I have to for the pleasure of adding that extra richness to a sauce or perfectly complementing a ripe tomato.

For an olive oil to be labelled extra virgin, the top designation, it must be derived entirely from the first pressing of the olives, which must take place within a few days of picking. Only cold pressing can be used to extract the oil. The very best extra virgin oils are also made from hand-picked olives, because bruises cause oxidation and acidity.

The oleic acid content of an oil is another factor in its quality: the lower the acid, the better the oil. When you buy an extra virgin oil, you know the oleic acid is in the 0.5 to 1 per cent range.

Tuscans have always claimed that their extra virgin oil is the best in Italy, and I agree. We prefer the vivid green oil pressed from underripe olives, because of its sharpness and piquancy. We love the richness of its fruit and its hints of herbs and pepper.

If you are a Tuscan, or want to be one for the day, you'll know that the flavour elements and colour of the oil vary, depending on the climate and soil where the trees grow. The delicate golden oils of Lucca are good with fish; the darker, fuller, intensely flavoured oils of the Chianti hills complement grilling vegetables and meat; and the salty, peppery oils of Tuscany's south coast go with fish and lighter meats such as chicken and veal. Colour alone is no indicator of the quality of an oil, although it may give a clue about the intensity of the flavour.

To add to the challenge of finding the right oil for the right dishes, you need to consider the label carefully. A truly Tuscan oil will have the words "Estate Bottled" and the place of origin. The good producers also put a "best before" date on the label. An extra virgin oil is at its best within a year of pressing, and better still, in the first six months of that year.

I suggest that you keep your oil stored in a place that is dry, cool and dark. Light will change the colour and lower the quality of the oil by breaking down the enzymes. I also suggest that you buy a small bottle if you don't use extra virgin oil often. Once you expose the oil to air, it will deteriorate quickly and become rancid if you leave it too long.

So use it! Have an oleic experience. Fresh extra virgin olive oil is a healthy way to enrich the flavour of almost any food.

PINZIMONIO

Pinzimonio comes from *pinzare*, "to pinch." It is a plate of vegetables with a small bowl of excellent olive oil mixed with lots of salt and an equal quantity of freshly ground black pepper. (I like two parts oil to one part combined salt and pepper.) You pinch a vegetable from the platter and dip it in the oil.

On the platter you will find whatever is in season: in spring, tiny raw baby artichokes and the first green onions, blanched wild asparagus and cooked new potatoes; in summer, raw radishes, carrots, sliced peppers, fennel, cucumber and blanched green beans.

Pinzimonio is made to accompany conversation – just a little pinch here and a little pinch there while you talk.

GRILLED PORCINI STEAKS

Ideally you want large mushrooms for this recipe, but with wild mushrooms you take what nature gives you. On your lucky day you might bring home some that are 5 to 7 inches (12 to 18 cm) wide. If so, serve one per person. If you come home with smaller ones, serve a few per person. This preparation also works well with portobello mushrooms, which you can find in the market without depending on luck at all.

INGREDIENTS

4	large, fresh porcini or portobello mushrooms, with stems

CAPS

	salt
	freshly ground black pepper
	extra virgin olive oil
1 clove	garlic, chopped
2	lemons for garnish

STEMS

2 tsp [10 mL]	olive oil
	salt
	freshly ground black pepper
2 Tbsp [30 mL]	dry white wine
1 clove	garlic, chopped
1 Tbsp [15 mL]	coarsely chopped parsley
	juice of 1/2 lemon

SERVES 4

PREPARATION

Brush the mushrooms to remove all traces of dirt. Separate the caps and stems, and set the stems aside.

Place the caps underside up on a grill pan. Sprinkle them with salt and pepper and drizzle with extra virgin olive oil. Sprinkle the chopped garlic over the caps. Let them rest for 30 minutes to absorb some of the oil.

Meanwhile, soak the stems in warm water for 10 minutes to soften and loosen any soil. Remove the stems from the water and quickly dry them with paper towels. Quarter the stems lengthwise (or halve them for smaller mushrooms).

In a cast-iron pan, heat the oil to medium heat. Add the stems, sprinkle them with salt and pepper and sauté them for 1 to 2 minutes. Add the white wine and continue to sauté until the wine has evaporated, about 2 minutes. Add the garlic and parsley and stir. Remove the pan from the heat.

Arrange the stems as a base on a serving platter or on individual plates. Squeeze 1/2 lemon over top.

To cook the mushroom caps, preheat the grill to hot. When the caps have marinated for 30 minutes, place them skin side down on the grill for 3 to 4 minutes, until the skin is nice and crisp.

Flip the caps over and cook them for a further 3 to 4 minutes. When they are still firm to the touch, remove them from the heat. They will be meaty and firm to the bite because most of the moisture will have evaporated. Arrange the caps on top of the stems. Drizzle on more extra virgin olive oil, add a grinding of black pepper, and serve another 1/2 lemon per person on the side.

VEGETARIAN CABBAGE ROLLS

The seafaring history of coastal Tuscany is reflected in the spice mixture that flavours these cabbage rolls. Cloves, cinnamon and coriander actually go back at least as far as Biblical times in various regions of Italy.

INGREDIENTS

12	large cabbage leaves
1/2 cup [125 mL]	olive oil
1/2 cup [125 mL]	finely chopped onion
1/2 cup [125 mL]	Arborio rice
4 cups [1 L]	vegetable broth
1/2 cup [125 mL]	chopped leeks
1/2 cup [125 mL]	cooked chickpeas
4 cloves	garlic, chopped
1/2 cup [125 mL]	finely chopped parsley
	juice of 1 lemon
	salt
	freshly ground black pepper
1/4 tsp [1 mL]	whole cloves
1/4 tsp [1 mL]	ground cinnamon
1/4 tsp [1 mL]	coriander seeds
1/4 tsp [1 mL]	chili seeds
1/2 cup [125 mL]	fresh tomatoes, peeled and chopped

SERVES 4

RECOMMENDED WINE
Vernaccia di San Gimignano

RECOMMENDED PRODUCERS
Riccardo Falchini-Il Casale, Teruzzi & Puthod, Le Colonne, Cecchi
The versatile Vernaccia of San Gimignano is as easily manipulated as New World Chardonnays. Clean and fresh, it is the ideal "lo-cal" wine to accompany this healthy dish.

PREPARATION

Clean the cabbage leaves and blanch them in boiling water until they are pliable enough to roll. Remove any stiff ribs. Drain the leaves and set them aside.

Heat 1/4 cup [60 mL] of the oil in a heavy pot and brown the onions. Stir in the rice and add the vegetable broth. Bring the broth to a boil, then simmer uncovered for about 20 minutes, cooking the rice until it is still a bit firm. Do not drain it.

Bring a small pot of water to a boil. Add the chopped leeks and boil briefly until they are tender, then drain them.

In a large bowl, mix the leeks, chickpeas, garlic, parsley, lemon juice, salt and pepper. Crush the cloves, cinnamon, coriander seeds and chili seeds together in a mortar or the small jar of a blender, and add them to the bowl. Stir in the rice and all its remaining broth, mixing well.

Preheat the oven to 375°F [190°C].

Coat a large baking dish with the remaining 1/4 cup [60 mL] oil. Stuff the cabbage leaves by laying them flat and placing a generous amount of filling toward one side. Roll from that side, tucking in the edges until you have a firm, solid roll. Arrange the rolls side by side in the baking dish.

Add enough cold water to come halfway up the rolls and sprinkle the chopped tomatoes over top. Season with salt and pepper. Bake for about 40 minutes or until tender. Remove from the oven and allow the rolls to rest for 20 minutes before serving, or cool to room temperature then chill, if you prefer to serve them cold.

Pasta, Rice, Polenta and Eggs

Pasta isn't served in quantity; it's the quality, and the balance with a little sauce to stimulate the appetite rather than to fill up the stomach.

TAGLIOLINI WITH ARUGULA

The name tagliolini comes from tagliare *– to cut – because it is traditionally made at home and cut by hand. Only recently has it been made commercially. The homemade variety is softer and more absorbent than the extruded commercial product, so it can't be served with a really liquid sauce. This dish is served around Easter, often with fried slices of sausage.*

INGREDIENTS

1 lb [500 g]	tagliolini pasta
	extra virgin olive oil
1 lb [500 g]	arugula
2 cloves	garlic
4 Tbsp [60 mL]	extra virgin olive oil
1/2 cup [125 mL]	coarsely chopped Parmesan or pecorino cheese
	pinch of minced fresh red chili
	OR a few drops of chili oil
	salt
	freshly ground black pepper

SERVES 4

PREPARATION

Cook pasta uncovered in a large pot of boiling salted water until al dente. Drain slightly, still leaving a small amount of water in the pasta. Drizzle a bit of olive oil on the pasta to keep the noodles from sticking together.

In a food processor put arugula, garlic, oil, cheese and chili and pulse until it is finely chopped. Add salt and pepper to taste. In a large skillet, toss the arugula mixture with the pasta and cook over medium heat until it is heated through. Remove it from the heat and serve it in a large bowl or platter.

Giovanna, chef and owner of Lido Ristorante in Quattro Strade near Pisa

Eggplant Stuffed with Tagliolini

When I first tasted this dish I was impressed at how each ingredient keeps its own personality, distinctive but balanced with the others. The flavours are very pure: the paper-thin egg noodles called tagliolini, sweet tomato and simply baked eggplant. This is a great dish to serve guests because it can be prepared ahead of time and heated in the oven at the last minute. It works as either a starter or a main dish. And, with the crispy-skinned eggplant making a bowl for the pasta and sauce, the presentation is beautiful.

Ingredients

2	large eggplants, at least 4 in. [10 cm] wide
	salt
	freshly ground black pepper
	extra virgin olive oil
1/2 lb [250 g]	tagliolini pasta, fresh and dry
	extra virgin olive oil

Fonduta di Pomodoro

1 lb [500 g]	fresh ripe tomatoes
4 cloves	garlic, chopped
1 Tbsp [15 mL]	chopped fresh basil
	salt
	freshly ground black pepper
1 Tbsp [15 mL]	extra virgin olive oil
4 Tbsp [60 mL]	freshly grated Parmesan cheese

Serves 4
Fonduta di Pomodoro yields
1 cup [250 mL]

Preparation

Preheat the oven to 375°F [190°C].

Cut the eggplants in half crosswise, and trim the rounded bottom and the blossom end to make them flat. Scoop out the white pulp, leaving a minimum of 1 in. [2.5 cm] on the base and sides to create a bowl. (You can save the pulp for some other purpose.) Keep the skin on. Place the eggplant bowls on a baking sheet, season with salt and pepper and drizzle with extra virgin olive oil. Bake them for 30 minutes and set aside to cool. If you are preparing the dish to eat immediately, leave the oven on.

In a large pot of boiling salted water, cook the pasta al dente, 5 to 7 minutes. Drain it and drizzle some extra virgin olive oil over the noodles to prevent sticking. Spread the noodles on a baking sheet and set them aside to cool.

Fonduta di Pomodoro

Cut the tomatoes into quarters. Put them in a large pot and bring them to a boil. Do not add oil! Cover and simmer gently for 20 to 30 minutes until the tomatoes are soft. Add garlic, basil, salt and pepper. Cover and simmer for another 10 minutes to let the basil and garlic soften.

Transfer the fonduta to a bowl by passing it through a fine food mill or sieve to achieve a thick, velvety sauce. Stir in extra virgin olive oil and set the fonduta aside to cool.

To assemble, place all 4 eggplant bowls in a large baking dish. In a separate bowl, mix and toss the tagliolini with the fonduta. Add the Parmesan cheese and toss again.

Fill each eggplant bowl with the mixture until the filling sits about 1/2 in. [1 cm] above the eggplant. If you will be cooking this dish later on, you can cover it at this point and keep it cold for several hours before finishing it in the oven at the last minute.

Heat the oven to 375°F [190°C] and bake the stuffed eggplant for 25 to 30 minutes.

Spaghetti from the Island of Elba

It's obvious that if you are surrounded by water the tendency is to use seafood whenever you can. Elba is a perfect example. Most pizzas and pastas include crustaceans or deep-water fish. Every islander claims to be the best seafood cook, but I'm not going to make any choices because I love to vacation there.

Ingredients

2 cloves	garlic, chopped
4 Tbsp [60 mL]	extra virgin olive oil
1 can	tomatoes (14 oz [398 mL])
1 can	oil-packed tuna, with oil (6 1/2 oz [184 g])
20	black kalamata olives, pitted and coarsely chopped
4	anchovy fillets, washed and chopped
1 tsp [5 mL]	chopped fresh oregano
2/3 cup [50 mL]	dry red wine
	freshly ground black pepper
1 lb [500 g]	spaghetti
4 Tbsp [60 mL]	grated pecorino cheese

Serves 4

Preparation

Sauté the garlic in the oil over medium-low heat. As soon as the garlic picks up a bit of colour, remove it from the pan. Add the tomatoes, tuna, olives, anchovies, oregano and wine. Increase the heat to medium and simmer uncovered for 10 minutes.

Pass the sauce through a food mill or pulse it a few times in a food processor, until it has a coarsely chopped texture. Add pepper to taste. You don't need to add salt because of the olives and the anchovies.

Boil the spaghetti in a large pot of salted water, drain well and serve it in bowls with the sauce and grated cheese.

Recommended Wine
Chianti Colli Fiorentini
Recommended Producers
Baggiolino, Lilliano, Lucignano, Torre a Decima
This humble Chianti is best drunk young. Its medium-bodied flavours of cherries, leather and earth and its dry finish make it an ideal light red for seafood.

PENNE IN A SPICY TOMATO SAUCE

Arrabbiato means angry, raging. In this recipe, chili oil provides the passion. I would rather use chili oil than dried red chili flakes because the flavour is cleaner and fresher. Chili-infused oils are available in specialty food stores or Asian markets, and you will find them handy for adding a dash of heat to any dish.

INGREDIENTS

3 Tbsp [50 mL]	extra virgin olive oil
6 cloves	garlic, minced
1	small red onion, finely diced
3 Tbsp [45 mL]	chopped Italian parsley
20	medium plum tomatoes, chopped
	OR two 28 oz [796 mL] cans
	of plum tomatoes
	salt
	freshly ground white pepper
	fresh chili oil to taste
2/3 lb [350 g]	penne pasta
	(about 1 cup [250 mL] per person)
1 Tbsp [15 mL]	olive oil

SERVES 4

PREPARATION

Heat the 3 Tbsp [50 mL] oil in a large saucepan over medium heat. Sauté the garlic, onion and parsley for 2 to 3 minutes, making sure that the garlic doesn't burn. Add the tomatoes and simmer uncovered for 20 minutes. Add the salt, pepper and chili oil to taste, and allow the chili flavour to cook into the sauce, about 5 minutes.

Bring a large pot of salted water to a boil. Add the penne and 1 Tbsp [15 mL] oil and boil uncovered for 6 to 8 minutes, or until al dente. Drain the noodles and transfer them to a serving platter.

Pour the sauce over the noodles and serve immediately.

RECOMMENDED WINE

Chianti Colline Pisane
Grown in the hills southeast of Pisa, this wine is considered the softest and lightest Chianti of all. It's best when drunk young and fruity, and with spicy pasta dishes like this one.

BAKED RIGATONI WITH HAM

Rigatoni is usually served with a chunky meat sauce that will stick to it and get into the holes. This is a good, rich example.

INGREDIENTS

6 oz [175 g]	cooked ham, diced
4 oz [125 g]	whole milk mozzarella, diced (about 3/4 cup [175 mL])
1 cup [250 mL]	cream
6 oz [175 g]	freshly grated Parmesan cheese (about 1 cup [250 mL])
1 lb [500 g]	rigatoni
2 Tbsp [25 mL]	butter

SERVES 4 TO 6

PREPARATION

Put the ham, mozzarella, cream and Parmesan in a heavy-bottomed pot. Cook over low heat at a gentle simmer for just a few minutes, until the cream is slightly reduced. Remove the sauce from the heat.

Drop the rigatoni into boiling salted water and boil uncovered until al dente. Drain immediately.

Preheat the oven to 400°F [200°C]. Grease a baking dish with the butter.

When the rigatoni is cooked, transfer it to the prepared baking dish, add the sauce and toss thoroughly. Bake it for 15 minutes, or until the top is browned and bubbling. Allow the dish to rest for a few minutes before serving.

RECOMMENDED WINE
Vernaccia di San Gimignano
RECOMMENDED PRODUCERS
Riccardo Falchini-Il Casale, Teruzzi & Puthod, Le Colonne, Cecchi

The Vernaccia grape of San Gimignano is an Old World answer to New World Chardonnay. Its clean, fresh, fruity flavours, with just a hint of almonds in the background, will pick up this creamy luncheon dish.

RISOTTO WITH LAMB SAUSAGE AND PEPPERS

*This robust dish is associated with the northwest region of Italy, Piedmont.
But in Tuscany we give it our own twist by adding more volume to the ingredients
that go in; the rice becomes the starch that accompanies the main flavours.
It also replaces bread, and not many things replace the bread on a Tuscan table.*

INGREDIENTS

1/4 cup [50 mL]	butter (1/2 stick)
1	yellow pepper, diced
1	red pepper, diced
2 cups [500 mL]	Arborio rice
1/4 cup [60 mL]	dry white wine
4 cups [1 L]	classic meat broth *(see page 157)* or chicken stock
	pinch of saffron
	salt
	freshly ground black pepper
1 lb [500 g]	lamb sausage, roughly chopped
2 Tbsp [25 mL]	brandy
4 Tbsp [60 mL]	grated Parmesan cheese

SERVES 6

PREPARATION

Choose a heavy-bottomed pot that is not too wide, so it retains the heat. Melt the butter over medium heat and sauté the peppers for about a minute. Add the rice and stir to coat all the grains. Stir in the wine and allow the alcohol to evaporate, stirring occasionally.

Add the broth and cook, stirring occasionally, until the rice is al dente, probably 20 to 25 minutes. In the last 2 minutes of cooking, stir in the saffron, salt and pepper. Cover the risotto and keep it warm on top of the stove.

Cook the chopped sausage in the brandy over medium heat. Once the alcohol has evaporated and the chunks of sausage are cooked, add the sausage and juices to the warm risotto. Salt to taste and add the Parmesan. Mix well and serve.

RECOMMENDED WINE
Brunello di Montalcino
RECOMMENDED PRODUCERS
Castello Banfi, Barbi, Biondi-Santi, Frescobaldi, Col d'Orcia

Open this wine before you prepare the meal and then sit back and enjoy a simple but sophisticated pairing of power and elegance.

Elba

If you had to choose a place of exile, wouldn't you choose one with perfect weather and a beautiful and varied landscape? Napoleon was lucky enough to be banished to Elba.

Isola d'Elba is the largest island of the Tuscan Archipelago, and the third largest island in Italy. On the ferry ride from the port of Piombino, you can watch the mountains and coastline of the mainland grow smaller, and in about an hour you find yourself in a mysterious new world of peaks and valleys, cliffs and canyons, crying seabirds, crystal sea and lush pine woods. On a three-hour drive around the island you will see so many different landscapes you might think you have been in several places at once. In some ways you will be right, because through its history Elba has been under the control of various Tuscan city-states as well as Spain, Turkey and France, and traces of all of them can still be found.

The island attracts all kinds of vacationers, from the yachters who invariably stop in as they cruise the Italian coast to the hikers who come to explore on foot. But its most famous visitor was not exactly a vacationer.

In the early nineteenth century, Napoleon Bonaparte created an empire that covered most of Europe. He was forced to abdicate in 1814 and was granted Elba as a sovereign principality.

Napoleon governed Elba for only 285 days, but in that short time he restored and added to an old palace, which is now known as Villa Bonaparte, and enriched the island's culture by commissioning works of art. All the while, he was plotting to escape and rebuild his empire. He did escape, and even seized the throne again, but his final defeat at Waterloo put an end to the Napoleonic Era.

The great poet Alessandro Manzoni wrote an elegy to this towering figure, which we learned by heart when I was in school:

The 5th of May
by Alessandro Manzoni

He was, and is no more.
Immobile, having sighed his last,
the mortal remains lie unremembering,
bereft of breath,
At the news, the earth
is stricken, unbelieving,
silent at the thought of his
last hour, this man of destiny,
nor does she know when
mortal feet shall tread again
and leave such footmarks
in her bloody dust.

That excerpt reminds me of the school excursion that took me to Elba for the first time. I was in grade two and had never been on a boat before. It was the longest trip of my life. As a young man I returned several years later on my Vespa, and recently I have been taking a short holiday on the island every year.

On a cold winter day in Vancouver, my mind takes me to my favourite little cove on Elba, where the water is turquoise, the sand white and the breeze sweet and light. A restaurant with a wood-fired oven serves a delicious seafood soup, which you eat at a table on the beach as your toes dig in the sand. This island is … what? Paradise? Heaven on earth? Banish yourself to Elba sometime, and you decide.

SAFFRON RISOTTO WITH PUMPKIN

Veal or beef marrow gives this risotto a rich, flavourful base. You can buy some bones and remove the raw marrow yourself, or simply ask the butcher to do it for you.

INGREDIENTS

1/4 cup [60 mL]	beef or veal marrow
3 Tbsp [50 mL]	olive oil
2	shallots, finely chopped
3/4 lb [375 g]	fresh pumpkin, peeled, seeded and finely diced
1/2 lb [250 g]	Arborio rice (1 1/4 cups [300 mL])
1/4 cup [60 mL]	white wine
4 cups [1 L]	chicken stock, hot
25–30	saffron threads
2 Tbsp [25 mL]	freshly grated Parmesan cheese
1 tsp [5 mL]	chopped parsley
1 Tbsp [15 mL]	butter
	salt
	white pepper

SERVES 4

PREPARATION

The night before you plan to make the risotto, put the marrow in a mixture of half water, half ice cubes. Leave the marrow submerged in the ice water overnight in the refrigerator; this will keep it firm and eliminate the taste of fat. When you are about to cook the risotto, remove the marrow from the water, dry it and dice it.

Heat the olive oil in a large, heavy pot over medium heat and sauté the shallots until they are transparent. Add the diced pumpkin and diced marrow and cook for 2 minutes.

Add the rice and stir frequently for 3 to 4 minutes. Pour in the wine and stir until it has evaporated. Add enough stock to cover the rice.

Put the saffron threads in the remaining stock. As the rice absorbs the liquid it is cooking in, gradually add more stock. Stir frequently until the additional stock is absorbed, and repeat until all the stock is used and the rice is creamy and cooked al dente or to your taste.

Before serving, stir in the Parmesan cheese, parsley, butter and salt and pepper.

RECOMMENDED WINE
Pinot Grigio
RECOMMENDED PRODUCERS
Banfi

Here's a refreshing, crisp, clean white with fine streaks of mineral/citrus flavours running through it. It will cut through the abundant flavours of the dish, all the while preparing the palate for the next delicious bite.

WILD RICE PILAF

In Tuscany we cooked this dish with wild rice for special occasions, but usually we used spelt (also called farro), which was more economical. Both wild rice and spelt have a nice nutty flavour, and they take the same time to cook. When I came to Canada I had trouble finding spelt, but it's now more common, especially in health food stores.

INGREDIENTS

1/2 cup [125 mL]	wild rice or spelt
1 cup [250 mL]	long-grain brown rice, rinsed and drained
1/2 cup [125 mL]	pine nuts
1/4 cup [50 mL]	raisins
2 Tbsp [30 mL]	extra virgin olive oil
3 cloves	garlic, minced
1/4 cup [50 mL]	minced fresh parsley
1/4 cup [50 mL]	minced fresh basil
4	green onions, sliced

SERVES 4 TO 6

PREPARATION

Cover the wild rice or spelt with cold water and soak it for 4 hours. Drain.

Bring 2 cups [500 mL] salted water to a boil. Add the wild rice or spelt and cook covered for 45 minutes or until tender.

In a separate pot, bring another 2 cups [500 mL] salted water to a boil. Add the brown rice, reduce the heat to low, cover and simmer for 45 minutes, or until the rice is tender.

While the rice is cooking, toast the pine nuts in a dry skillet over medium-low heat, shaking the pan often until the pine nuts just begin to colour, 5 to 8 minutes. Immediately remove them from the heat. When the wild rice is cooked, drain it and combine it with the cooked brown rice.

Mix the pine nuts, raisins, olive oil, garlic, parsley, basil and green onions, and stir into the rice. Serve the pilaf hot as a side dish.

AUNT LALLA'S LASAGNA

Our annual family trip was a four-hour train ride to see Aunt Lalla. The main point was to eat our fill of her delicious lasagna, but for each of us kids she also had a toy or gift. My older brother's toy always seemed better than mine, so I spent the trip home plotting, dealing and fighting to get it away from him, to the annoyance of our parents. I don't know whether it's the lasagna or the toys that make me remember so well, but they're both good memories. I suggest that you make fresh pasta for best results, and also to please my Aunt Lalla.

INGREDIENTS

FRESH PASTA

4 cups [1 L]	all-purpose flour
3 cups [750 mL]	semolina flour
1/4 cup [60 mL]	unsalted butter (1/2 stick), at room temperature
6	eggs
	pinch of salt
1/4 cup [60 mL]	Vin Santo or other sweet white wine

SERVES 12

INGREDIENTS

MEAT SAUCE

2 Tbsp [30 mL]	olive oil
2 lbs [1 kg]	lean ground beef
1/2 cup [125 mL]	dry white wine
1	large red or white onion, coarsely chopped
2	medium carrots, coarsely chopped
1 1/4 lbs [625 g]	peeled fresh tomatoes, coarsely chopped
	OR one 19 oz [540 mL] can with juice
1 tsp [5 mL]	chopped fresh sage
1 tsp [5 mL]	chopped fresh rosemary
1 tsp [5 mL]	chopped fresh chili pepper
	salt
	freshly ground black pepper
2 cups [500 mL]	chicken or beef stock
2 Tbsp [30 mL]	tomato paste
2 Tbsp [30 mL]	extra virgin olive oil

WHITE SAUCE

4 cups [1 L]	partially skimmed milk
1/3 cup [75 mL]	unsalted butter
1/2 cup [125 mL]	all-purpose flour
	salt
	freshly ground white pepper
	freshly grated nutmeg
1 cup [250 mL]	grated Parmesan cheese

RECOMMENDED WINE
Chianti

RECOMMENDED PRODUCERS
Frescobaldi, Selvapiana, Travignoli
Rufina may be the smallest zone in Chianti, but it produces big wines. This robust, fruity red mixes dried cherry and earth flavours in equal measure.

PREPARATION

To prepare the fresh pasta, put both kinds of flour on a smooth surface, making a well in the centre. Put the rest of the pasta ingredients into the well and work everything together with your hands, gradually mixing in flour until the dough is uniformly combined (you probably won't need all the flour). If the dough is sticky, gradually add more flour, a bit at a time (or you can use a dough mixer). When the dough is no longer sticky, stop incorporating the flour.

Knead the dough as fast as you can until it is smooth and silky, 8 to 10 minutes. Then, using a pasta maker or a rolling pin, roll the dough into thin layers – "the thinner the better," said my aunt with a master's authority. Cut the pasta into approximately 4 in. [10 cm] squares.

MEAT SAUCE

For the meat sauce, heat the oil in a deep, heavy-bottomed 12 in. [30 cm] pot and brown the ground beef until all the liquid disappears. Add the wine and let it evaporate. Then add the onion, carrots, tomatoes, sage, rosemary, chili pepper and salt and pepper. Continue to cook on medium heat for 30 to 40 minutes. Add the stock and cook for another 30 minutes, stirring frequently to ensure the sauce doesn't stick to the bottom of the pot. When the sauce looks thick but not dry, add the tomato paste (the best brand you can find); this will impart a good lustrous red colour. Put the sauce aside to rest for 30 minutes, and drizzle a little extra virgin olive oil over the top.

WHITE SAUCE

To make the white sauce, heat the milk to just below the boiling point and remove from heat. Meanwhile, melt the butter over medium heat in a heavy-bottomed pot large enough to contain 4 cups [1 L] of milk. Mix the flour into the butter and stir over the heat for 1 or 2 minutes, until the mixture softens and spreads out. Add the warm milk, salt, pepper and nutmeg. Bring to a slow boil until the sauce is thick and smooth. Stir often. When thickened, remove the sauce from heat and set aside.

ASSEMBLY

Cook the pasta in lots of boiling salted water. If you make it fresh, it should take only 1 to 2 minutes to cook al dente. With dried pasta it will take 10 to 12 minutes. Then, drain and rinse the pasta with cold water to prevent sticking.

Preheat the oven to 350°F [180°C].

Spread the bottom of a 9 x 15 in. [23 x 38 cm] glass or enamel pan with a little of the meat sauce. Place a layer of the pasta on top, then another 1/4 of the meat sauce, followed by 1/4 of the white sauce.

Sprinkle with 1/4 of the grated Parmesan cheese. Make 3 more layers in that order, then bake for at least 30 minutes or until the top layers are browned and very crispy.

FLORENTINE CANNELLONI

Spinach is much loved in Florence because it grows in abundance in the area. This classic recipe needs no improvement. People always try to mess with it – adding tomatoes or peppers or whatever – but no one from Florence would be impressed. So be a Florentine – try this cannelloni as it was meant to be. You will find it a rich and gratifying dish, successful at any gathering as either a first course or a main dish. It also freezes well, so you can cook the whole thing and freeze half.

INGREDIENTS

12	fresh pasta sheets, 4 x 8 in. [10 x 20 cm]

SPINACH AND CHEESE FILLING

6 bunches	spinach, washed and stemmed
1 Tbsp [15 mL]	unsalted butter
1 Tbsp [15 mL]	olive oil
2	large onions, finely diced
1	large carrot, finely diced
6 cloves	garlic, crushed
1 cup [250 mL]	freshly grated Parmesan cheese
1 cup [250 mL]	ricotta cheese
1/2 cup [125 mL]	fine fresh breadcrumbs
1 tsp [5 mL]	freshly grated nutmeg
1/4 cup [50 mL]	dry white wine
	zest of 2 lemons
	coarse salt
	freshly ground white pepper
	pinch of cayenne pepper
4	eggs

SERVES 12

THICK WHITE SAUCE

4 Tbsp [60 mL]	butter
1/2 cup [125 mL]	flour
2 cups [500 mL]	milk, hot
1/4 cup [50 mL]	freshly grated Parmesan cheese
4 sprigs	parsley, chopped
	freshly ground white pepper

RECOMMENDED WINE
Chianti
RECOMMENDED PRODUCERS
Frescobaldi, Selvapiana, Travignoli
For a robust, fruity red that will stand up to both the spinach and the rich cheese, look to a Chianti from the hills east of Florence.

Silvano of Le Fonticine Ristorante in Florence

PREPARATION

Bring a large pot of salted water to a boil and cook the pasta sheets, one at a time, for 2 to 3 minutes, or until al dente. Lay the cooked sheets individually on towels to dry for a couple of minutes.

SPINACH AND CHEESE FILLING

Bring another large pot of salted water to a boil and blanch the spinach until it is just wilted. Drain it well, then chop it and put it in a large bowl.

Heat the butter and oil in a skillet over medium heat and sauté the onions until they are soft. Then add the carrots and garlic and sauté for about 5 minutes or until the carrots are soft. Add the mixture to the spinach and combine well.

Now add the Parmesan, ricotta, bread-crumbs, nutmeg, wine, lemon zest, salt, pepper and cayenne. Mix well, taste and adjust the seasonings if necessary. Add the eggs and mix well.

Divide the filling among the pasta sheets. Roll the pasta around the filling, leaving enough of a border for the pasta to overlap and form a seam when it is rolled into a tube.

THICK WHITE SAUCE

To make the white sauce, melt the butter in a small pot over medium heat. Reduce the heat to medium-low and stir in the flour. Cook the roux for 3 to 5 minutes, mashing it with a fork or the back of a spoon to cook all of the flour. Don't let it brown. When the roux turns shiny and softens a bit it is ready. Whisk in 1/4 of the hot milk at a time. Simmer, stirring or whisking, until the sauce thickens. It will almost be a paste at this point, but the liquids in the dish will thin the sauce some-what during baking.

Preheat the oven to 350°F [180°C].

ASSEMBLY

Spread 1/3 of the white sauce over the bottom of a baking dish large enough to hold all the cannelloni in one layer. (If the white sauce is too solid to spread, add a bit of whipping cream.) Place the cannelloni in the baking dish seam side down, and cover with the remaining white sauce. Sprinkle the Parmesan over the top.

Bake the cannelloni for about 30 minutes, or until the white sauce is golden brown and bubbling. Before serving, sprinkle with some chopped parsley and a bit of freshly ground white pepper.

Making dough for pasta.

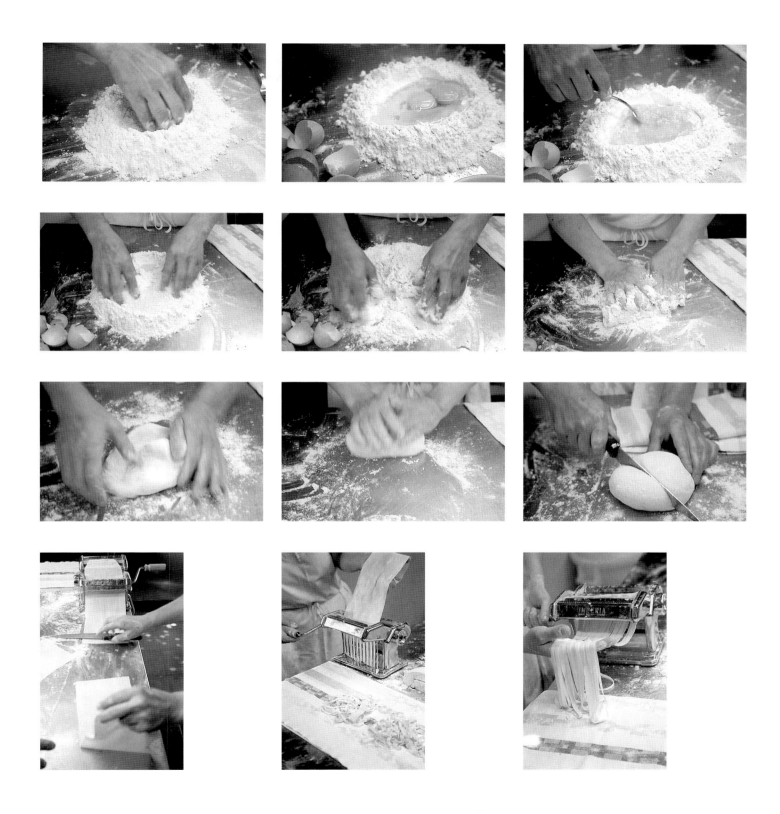

GNOCCHI

A light touch is the secret to good gnocchi. If you overmix them or handle them too much you'll stimulate the gluten in the flour and they will become heavy. This recipe can be doubled, and the finished gnocchi can be frozen. Try them with ragù *(page 163), gorgonzola sauce, pesto (page 162) or tomato sauce (page 164), and a sprinkling of Parmesan cheese.*

INGREDIENTS

2 lbs [1 kg]	Yukon Gold potatoes, skins on
2 cups [500 mL]	flour
1	egg
1 Tbsp [15 mL]	freshly grated Parmesan cheese
	pinch of salt

SERVES 6

PREPARATION

Boil potatoes until tender, and drain. While the potatoes are still warm, remove the skins, either by rubbing with a cloth or peeling with a knife.

Pour the flour on a clean surface and make a well in the middle. Press the peeled potatoes through a ricer into the well in the flour. Create a small well in the potatoes and pour in the egg, cheese and salt.

Using your hands, first incorporate the egg, cheese and salt into the potatoes, then gradually incorporate flour until the mixture reaches a firm, doughlike consistency. You might not need all the flour. Form the dough into a ball.

Cut the ball into quarters, and roll each quarter into an 18 in. [45 cm] long sausage shape by working from the middle out to the ends. Cut off 3/4 in. [2 cm] pieces on the diagonal, flicking them off the knife as you go. Keep them separate so they won't stick together. Allow the gnocchi to rest for 15 minutes.

Bring a very large pot of salted water to a boil. Throw in a few gnocchi at a time. When cooked, in about 3 to 4 minutes, they will float to the surface. Remove them immediately with a slotted spoon, drain and keep warm until serving.

POLENTA

All winter, polenta is the starch that coats your stomach and fills you up. It is mostly served to complement game dishes. We made it in a big pot in the fireplace, and as we sat around the fire to keep warm, whoever was closest stirred the polenta until they got too hot and had to back away. Now I see people paying a lot of money to buy Tuscan farmhouses, trying to revive that kind of experience, which for us was simple survival.

INGREDIENTS

4 cups [1 L]	water
1 tsp [5 mL]	salt
1 cup [250 mL]	cornmeal

SERVES 4

PREPARATION

Bring the salted water to a boil. Pour in the cornmeal in a thin steady stream, stirring constantly with a whisk or a wooden spoon. Reduce heat to just under medium.

Keep stirring in the same direction until there are no lumps, then cook uncovered at a low simmer for 45 minutes. Stir the polenta frequently, remembering to keep stirring in the same direction so you won't create lumps. When it is creamy in texture and solid, it is ready to serve.

Spoon the polenta onto plates and top with cheese or a favourite sauce. If you would rather serve it in slices, smooth the polenta into an oiled flat pan and allow it to set for 15 minutes. Then cut it into whatever shape you wish.

RED PEPPER, BASIL AND GOAT CHEESE FRITTATA

The difference between an omelet and a frittata is that an omelet folds around the other ingredients, so you taste the egg separately. In a frittata, the eggs become flavoured with the other ingredients because they're all mixed together. The frittata is also cooked on both sides, for a torte-like consistency. In Italy, you'll find seasonally inspired frittatas served at any meal, any time of day.

INGREDIENTS

1/2	medium red bell pepper
4	eggs
	salt
	freshly ground black pepper
3	fresh basil leaves, chopped
1 tsp [5 mL]	olive oil
2 oz [60 g]	fresh goat cheese, cubed

SERVES 2

PREPARATION

Roast the red pepper over a flame or under the broiler until the skin is blackened and the pepper is limp. Let the pepper cool in a paper bag, then slide off the blackened skin. Coarsely chop the roasted pepper.

In a large bowl, mix the eggs, salt, black pepper and basil and set aside. You don't want to beat the eggs and incorporate a lot of air because the frittata will burn too easily.

In a medium non-stick skillet, heat the olive oil over medium heat, and sauté the roasted pepper for 3 to 4 minutes; then add it along with the goat cheese to the egg mixture. Stir well.

Pour the egg mixture into the skillet. The less you disturb the frittata as it cooks, the better. If the bottom seems to be browning too quickly, reduce the heat. Cook the frittata for 3 to 4 minutes, or until it is solid and a little creamy in the centre. To cook the other side, slide the frittata onto a plate and flip it back into the pan. Or, put it in the oven at 375°F [190°C] until the desired firmness is reached.

ASPARAGUS FRITTATA

I love frittata, especially when spring arrives and tiny wild asparagus appear in the fields among the chicory and nettles. My mother always shaved some fresh pecorino cheese on top of this frittata and served it with a garlic bruschetta on the side. Brava, Mamma. *I can still taste it.*

INGREDIENTS

1 lb [500 g]	thin asparagus (wild, if possible)
4	eggs
2 Tbsp [30 mL]	freshly grated Parmesan cheese
	salt
	freshly ground black pepper
1 Tbsp [15 mL]	olive oil

SERVES 2

PREPARATION

Bring a large pot of salted water to a boil. Break off the woody parts of the asparagus stalks and discard. Boil the stalks until they are tender but still firm. The time will vary according to the thickness of the stalks.

Beat the eggs well and mix in the asparagus, Parmesan, salt and pepper.

Heat the olive oil in a medium non-stick skillet over medium heat. Pour in the egg mixture and cook it until the eggs are set about halfway through.

Reduce the heat if the frittata is browning too quickly on the bottom. With one or two flexible spatulas, ease the frittata halfway out of the pan and gently flip it over completely. Or, slide it onto a plate and flip it back into the pan. The asparagus will help keep it together. Cook the frittata until is solid, but not dry.

RICE FRITTATA

This frittata tastes wonderful warm or cold. A bit of warm tomato sauce (see page 63 or 164) complements it well. It often appears, warm or at room temperature, cut in small wedges on an antipasto platter.

INGREDIENTS

1 cup [250 mL]	raw Arborio rice
	OR 2 cups [500 mL] cooked rice
3 Tbsp [45 mL]	butter
4	eggs
	handful of parsley, chopped
	salt
	freshly ground black pepper

SERVES 2

PREPARATION

To cook the rice, bring 8 cups [2 L] salted water to a boil. Add the rice and boil uncovered for 15 to 20 minutes, or until the rice is al dente. Drain it well and let it cool a bit before you make the frittata.

Melt the butter in a large non-stick skillet over medium-low heat. Beat the eggs gently and mix in the cooked rice, parsley and salt and pepper. Pour the egg mixture into the melted butter in the pan. When the eggs are solid halfway through and the surface is still a bit runny, use one or two flexible egg turners to flip it. Or, slide it onto a plate or the lid of the pan, then flip it back into the pan. Cook it for another 1 or 2 minutes, just until it is firm all through.

Cut it in wedges and serve either hot, warm or room temperature.

ARTICHOKE SOUFFLÉ

This soufflé is more sturdy than most, so you don't have to time your entire meal around it.

INGREDIENTS

8	medium artichokes
	juice of 1 lemon
3 Tbsp [45 mL]	butter
1 Tbsp [15 mL]	butter
1 Tbsp [15 mL]	flour
1 cup [250 mL]	milk, hot
1/2 cup [125 mL]	freshly grated Parmesan cheese
3	eggs, separated
1 Tbsp [15 mL]	butter
2 Tbsp [25 mL]	dry breadcrumbs

SERVES 6

PREPARATION

Wash the artichokes and cut the top half off each one. Trim off anything that is not light green, and remove the fuzzy choke. Dice the artichokes and immediately put them in a pot of salted water. Cover the pot, bring the water to a boil and cook the artichokes for about 10 minutes, or until tender. Drain them and squeeze on the lemon juice.

Heat the 3 Tbsp [45 mL] butter in a small skillet over medium heat and sauté the artichokes for 5 minutes. Purée the artichokes in a food processor or blender until they are smooth.

Preheat the oven to 375°F [190°C].

Make a white sauce by heating the 1 Tbsp [15 mL] butter in a small pot and whisking in the flour. Whisk the roux over medium heat for 2 to 3 minutes, or until it lightens in colour. Whisk in the hot milk a bit at a time and continue whisking until the sauce thickens.

Remove the sauce from the heat and add the puréed artichokes and Parmesan cheese. Beat the egg yolks and stir them into the sauce. If the sauce is still very hot, stir a spoonful of it into the egg yolks before you add them.

Whip the egg whites to soft peaks and gently fold them into the sauce.

Butter an 8 in. [2.5 L] soufflé dish and coat the inside with a thin layer of breadcrumbs (or do the same with 6 ramekins). Pour in the egg mixture. Place the dish in a baking pan half filled with hot water. Bake for 35 to 45 minutes, or until the soufflé is slightly brown on top.

Remove the pan from the oven and let the soufflé rest in the water bath for 5 to 10 minutes. Remove the soufflé dish and dry it off.

To serve, run a knife around the edge of the soufflé dish, then upend the soufflé onto a serving dish.

FISH AND SHELLFISH

In the summer heat we think of fish and shellfish
for their lightness and for our love and respect for the sea.

COD, POTATO AND ARTICHOKE CASSEROLE

I have cravings for casserole dishes, but it's not too often you get casseroles in restaurants or when you're invited for dinner. They seem to be thought of as unimpressive, but how can you not love a dish where everything is blessed with harmony? Made with fish or vegetables, meat or fowl, casseroles warm your heart, and they're so easy to prepare.

INGREDIENTS

4	large fresh artichokes
	OR 14 oz [298 mL] canned or frozen artichoke hearts, cut in thin wedges
	juice of 1 lemon
2 tsp [10 mL]	salt
1 1/2 lbs [750 g]	cod fillets
	salt
	freshly ground black pepper
5–6	medium Yukon Gold potatoes
2	medium onions
	freshly ground black pepper
1/2 tsp [2 mL]	ground nutmeg
4 Tbsp [60 mL]	butter (1/2 stick)
1 1/2 cups [375 mL]	milk
1 cup [250 mL]	chicken stock
4 Tbsp [60 mL]	freshly grated Parmesan cheese
	chopped parsley for garnish

SERVES 4

RECOMMENDED WINE
Sauvignon Blanc
RECOMMENDED PRODUCERS
Avignonesi (Il Vignola), Banfi (Serena), Castellare di Castellina (Spartito) Sauvignon Blanc is hardly a classic Tuscan variety, but in the right spot and with the right food it not only works, it can be magic. Seconds anyone?

PREPARATION

To prepare fresh artichokes, trim off the stems, spiky tips and any brown outer leaves, and squeeze lemon juice over the exposed tops and bottoms as you trim.

Stand the artichokes upright in a stainless steel or enamel saucepan large enough to contain them and cover them three-quarters with water. Add salt to the water and bring to a boil. Reduce the heat and simmer the artichokes for 25 to 35 minutes, until they are tender but firm. Drain them and rinse under cold running water. Set them aside and allow them to cool.

When the artichokes are cool, halve them and clean them of the spiny parts and hairy choke. Discard the leaves. Cut the hearts into thin wedges. Set aside.

Remove any pin bones from the cod and cut it into 1 in. [2.5 cm] cubes. Rinse the cubes of cod under cold running water and pat dry with paper towels. Season with salt and pepper and set aside.

Peel and thinly slice the potatoes, and keep them in a pot of cold water until you need them, then drain. (This step lets the potatoes re-absorb some of the moisture they've lost during storage.) Thinly slice the onions and separate them into rings.

Preheat oven to 400°F [200°C].

Butter a 12 x 8 in. [30 x 20 cm] glass or enamel baking dish and put in a layer of potatoes, onions, artichokes and cod, in that order. Season with salt, pepper and nutmeg and dab with butter. Repeat for each layer – you should end up with four layers.

Mix milk and chicken stock and pour over the ingredients in the baking dish. Sprinkle with Parmesan.

Bake for 30 to 40 minutes. Remove from the oven and sprinkle with parsley. Serve the casserole directly from the baking dish into individual bowls.

COD GRILLED WITH GARLIC AND OIL

It used to be a religious requirement to eat meatless meals on Friday, but now it's a tradition. On Friday, every city market is still packed with fresh fish. Cod and other cold-water fish have some fat and can stand up to grilling. Apart from the marinating time, this dish is very quick to prepare.

INGREDIENTS

4	fillets fresh cod, about 8–10 oz [250–350 g] each
	salt
	freshly ground black pepper
4 cloves	garlic, finely chopped
4 Tbsp [60 mL]	extra virgin olive oil
1 tsp [5 mL]	chili oil
1	lemon
4 Tbsp [60 mL]	dry white wine
	extra virgin olive oil for garnish
	lemon for garnish
1 sprig	parsley, finely chopped, for garnish

SERVES 4

PREPARATION

Place the cod fillets in a pan large enough to hold them all in one layer. Generously season with salt and pepper. Sprinkle the garlic evenly over the fish. Drizzle on the olive oil and the chili oil. Squeeze the lemon over the fish and sprinkle on the wine.

Let the fish marinate in the fridge for about 1 hour.

Heat the barbecue or grill to medium and oil the racks so the fish won't stick. Grill the fish for about 5 minutes on each side, moving it around from time to time. When it is just firm to the touch, it is done.

Transfer the fish to a warm platter or individual plates and finish with a drizzle of oil and a sprinkling of lemon juice and chopped parsley.

RECOMMENDED WINE
Galestro
RECOMMENDED PRODUCERS
Rocca delle Macìe, Cecchi, Antinori
Dry and lively green-apple fruit punctuates the crisp tart finish of this quaffer.
It's the perfect foil for grilled fish drizzled with olive oil.

Scorfano al pomodoro piccante

BAKED RED SNAPPER IN AROMATIC TOMATO SAUCE

Pisa's history as a major sea power is evident in its cooking. Pisan sailors brought back cumin, turmeric, yogurt and other North African and Middle Eastern flavours, and incorporated them in dishes like this one. The sauce is great on its own over plain spaghetti.

INGREDIENTS

AROMATIC TOMATO SAUCE

4 Tbsp [60 mL]	olive oil
3 cloves	garlic, finely chopped
1 Tbsp [15 mL]	fennel seed, crushed
1 tsp [5 mL]	finely chopped fresh chili
6–8	pitted black olives, crushed
8	large tomatoes, chopped
1 Tbsp [15 mL]	ground cumin
1 tsp [5 mL]	ground turmeric
3/4 cup [175 mL]	fish stock or water
1/2 cup [125 mL]	plain yogurt
1	whole red snapper or other small white fish, about 1 1/2 lbs [750 g]
	salt
	freshly ground black pepper
	juice of 1 lemon

SERVES 4

PREPARATION

Preheat the oven to 450°F [230°C].

Heat 3 Tbsp [45 mL] of the oil in a sauté pan over medium heat. Sauté the garlic, fennel seed, chili and olives for 2 minutes. Add the tomatoes, cumin and turmeric and simmer uncovered for 10 minutes.

While the sauce is simmering, prepare the fish. Clean and scale the whole fish, then make 3 or 4 diagonal slashes about 1 in. [2.5 cm] deep in the thicker parts. These cuts will allow the fish to absorb the flavour and cook more evenly.

Place the whole fish in a lightly greased baking dish. Season it with salt, pepper and lemon juice and cover it with foil. Bake for 30 minutes, or until the thicker part of the flesh flakes easily when tested with a knife.

When the sauce has simmered for 10 minutes, add the fish stock and cook covered for 20 minutes more. Remove the cover and simmer for 5 minutes more to thicken the sauce.

To serve, place the fish on a warm platter. Remove the sauce from the heat, and stir in the yogurt thoroughly just before serving. Pour the sauce over the fish and serve it immediately.

RECOMMENDED WINE
Vernaccia di San Gimignano
RECOMMENDED PRODUCERS
Riccardo Falchini-Il Casale, Teruzzi & Puthod, Le Colonne, Cecchi
Clean, fresh, fruity flavours work well with the rich snapper meat and the acidity in the tomato sauce.

La Versilia

Continuing on from the Côte d'Azur and the Riviera, La Versilia is the northwestern coastline of Tuscany, home of one of the biggest fleets of fish boats – and one of the biggest fleets of Ferraris and Mercedes Benzes – along the Mediterranean. If you don't know the name, it's because you're not Italian.

La Versilia is home to a seafaring people who have historically looked to the sea for food and for expansion. Like the Pisans, they sailed and traded throughout the Mediterranean and the Middle East.

From sailors, they became merchants. Many of them made fortunes and built villas on beautiful coves and beaches on the coast. Wealth brings wealth, and for a long time this area has attracted the Florentines and Milanese with money to spend on elegant summer homes.

This is the playground of Italy, where people go to enjoy some entertainment and high living. Especially in the summer, the place buzzes: the nightlife never stops; there are clubs and shows everywhere. The style is lavish, with fine stores and the largest concentration of yacht builders in Italy – and possibly the world. Most of the sleek Italian yachts that sail along this coast were built here too. (The English poet Percy Bysshe Shelley drowned just north of La Versilia when his boat sank. I don't know if it was built locally. Probably not!)

La Versilia isn't just for wealth and recreation. From the long, lovely beaches you can see the Apuan Alps, which look like snow-capped peaks. Actually the white areas are marble quarries, the source of the solid white Carrara marble that artists, such as Michelangelo, have carved into sculptures that seem to live and breathe. This is the region of chestnut trees, *castagni*. It has given the rest of Tuscany most of the chestnut dishes that are so cherished in the winter. And Tuscany's largest fishing fleets, based in Viareggio and Livorno, range as far as Corsica to catch the fish that will be sold in markets throughout Tuscany.

If you love food, this is where you're likely to find the best seafood restaurants in Tuscany – one of my favourites is Lorenzo in Forte dei Marmi. Young chefs and restaurant workers from all over Italy flock to La Versilia for experience in food and service. If you're in the business, it is almost a necessary destination to build yourself an impressive résumé.

I spent three months there when I was just starting out, and I think that meeting the vacationers and wealthy Italians who populate La Versilia in the summer gave me the energy to look across the sea and aspire to visiting the rest of the world. Or maybe it was the seafaring ways of the original mariners. In La Versilia, the influence of both is strong.

SIMPLE SKATE

Skate day was Friday, and I looked forward to it. I still enjoy it to this day. This is a much lighter treatment than the usual browned butter and caper sauce. Steamed potatoes, beans and carrots keep it simple.

INGREDIENTS

1 lb [500 g]	skate wing, side bones removed
4 cups [1 L]	water
1/2	medium onion, chopped
1/2	medium carrot, chopped
1 stalk	celery, chopped
1	leek, white part only, washed and chopped
	juice of 1/2 lemon
1/2 cup [125 mL]	white wine vinegar
1	bay leaf
	salt
10	peppercorns, crushed
1 sprig	parsley
1 sprig	fresh thyme
	extra virgin olive oil
	juice of 1/2 lemon
	chopped parsley for garnish

SERVES 2

PREPARATION

Wash the skate under cold running water and cut it in 2 portions.

Make a court bouillon by putting the water, vegetables, lemon juice, vinegar and seasonings into a sauté pan large enough to hold the fish pieces without overlapping. Bring the liquid to a boil, then lower the heat a bit. Place the skate in the court bouillon and keep it at a low boil for 15 to 20 minutes. As soon as the rows of flesh start to separate, the fish is done.

Serve the skate with a bit of the court bouillon in a shallow bowl. Drizzle it with some extra virgin olive oil and lemon juice and sprinkle on some chopped parsley.

RECOMMENDED WINE
Chardonnay
RECOMMENDED PRODUCERS
Castellare di Castellina (Canonico), Ruffino Libaio, San Felice (Capitolare del Muschio), Terrabianca (Piano della Capella), Tua Rita (Sileno)

Tuscan Chardonnay is richer than its northern Italian counterparts but it still manages to retain a light, vibrant, fresh style that makes it the choice for simply prepared seafood.

TUNA WITH SPINACH

Tuna is a very delicate fish; it can become as dry as sawdust if it's overcooked. It is best rare or medium-rare. So please use your own judgement for cooking times.

INGREDIENTS

6 bunches	fresh spinach, washed and stemmed
2 Tbsp [30 mL]	extra virgin olive oil
4	fresh tuna fillets, 8–10 oz [250–300 g] each
2	small shallots, finely diced
2 cloves	garlic, crushed
2 Tbsp [30 mL]	chopped fennel tops or dill
1/2 cup [125 mL]	tomato sauce
2 Tbsp [30 mL]	capers
2 Tbsp [30 mL]	chopped parsley
	juice of 2 lemons
	salt
	freshly ground black pepper
1 1/2 tsp [7 mL]	butter
1 1/2 tsp [7 mL]	extra virgin olive oil

SERVES 4

RECOMMENDED WINE
Pinot Noir
RECOMMENDED PRODUCER
Banfi
Tuscan Pinot Noir is rare but worth finding. The Pinot fruit counterbalances the richness of the tuna so all you have to do is enjoy the meal.

PREPARATION

Blanch the spinach in boiling salted water until it is wilted. Drain it well by putting it in a sieve and pressing it with a wooden spoon. Set aside.

Heat 1 Tbsp [15 mL] of the oil in a skillet over medium heat. Fry the tuna fillets for 3 to 4 minutes on each side. They should still be rare and should give a bit when touched, because they will cook for another few minutes in the sauce. Set the tuna aside and keep warm.

Heat the remaining 1 Tbsp [15 mL] of the oil in the same skillet; when it is hot, sauté the shallots, garlic and fennel tops for 2 to 3 minutes. Add the tomato sauce and bring it to a slow boil. Add the capers, parsley, lemon juice, salt and pepper and cook a further 3 to 4 minutes. Check the sauce for seasonings, then add the tuna and cook for another 2 to 3 minutes.

Meanwhile, heat the butter and oil in a large skillet over medium heat, and quickly sauté the spinach for about a minute. Season it with salt and pepper.

Spread the spinach on a platter and arrange the tuna on top. Cover half of each tuna fillet with sauce and let the sauce run down into the spinach. Serve immediately.

Vongole alla livornese

LIVORNESE STEAMED CLAMS

In Livorno, almost all the food involves some combination of wine and tomato.
This dish is a fine example. It can also be made with mussels – just leave out
the lemon thyme because they don't go together well.

INGREDIENTS

6 lbs [2.7 kg]	fresh clams
2 Tbsp [25 mL]	extra virgin olive oil
1/2 cup [125 mL]	finely chopped onions
2 cloves	garlic, coarsely chopped
2 sprigs	parsley, finely chopped
1 sprig	lemon thyme, finely chopped
	dash of cayenne pepper
1 cup [250 mL]	dry white wine
2 cups [500 mL]	cold water
8	medium ripe tomatoes, skinned, seeded and julienned
1 Tbsp [15 mL]	tomato paste
	salt
	freshly ground black pepper
2	lemons, cut in wedges, for garnish

SERVES 4

PREPARATION

If you feel any sand on the clams, brush them or wash them in cold running water in a strainer. Discard any clams that are open and do not close when they are poked.

In a large soup pot, heat the oil over medium heat. Sauté the onions and garlic for a couple of minutes until they become soft but not browned. Add the clams, and toss them gently with the onions.

Add parsley, lemon thyme, cayenne, wine, water, tomatoes, tomato paste and salt and pepper. Cook uncovered for 3 to 4 minutes, then put the lid on the pot and finish cooking for another 3 to 4 minutes, or until all the clam shells have opened.

Heap the clams in a serving bowl and top with the juices. Garnish with lemon wedges.

RECOMMENDED WINE
Chardonnay/Pinot Grigio blends
RECOMMENDED PRODUCERS
Ruffino (Libaio), Querciabella (Batar)
Both wines offer refreshingly, clean, crisp flavours with elements of mineral and citrus to play against the sweet meat of clams and mussels.

MARIETTA'S SALT COD

You would have a hard time finding an Italian who doesn't love this divine dish. It is something to share with friends and neighbours, served on a big platter in the middle of the table. In fact, I have never seen this baccalà *served on individual plates.*

INGREDIENTS

6 pieces	salt cod fillet, about 8 oz [250 g] each
1/2 cup [125 mL]	flour
1	egg
	freshly ground black pepper
	sunflower oil for frying
1 Tbsp [15 mL]	olive oil
2	medium onions, sliced
1 lb [500 g]	tomatoes, peeled, seeded and chopped
2 cloves	garlic, chopped
	handful of parsley

SERVES 6

RECOMMENDED WINE
Galestro
RECOMMENDED PRODUCERS
Rocca delle Macìe, Cecchi, Antinori
A delicate fruity nose, lively green-apple fruit and a crisp tart finish – these are just the ticket to cut through the batter and marry with the cod.

PREPARATION

To desalt the cod, put it in a large pot and fill the pot to the brim with water. Place the pot under a thin stream of running water for 10 to 12 hours. The running water will constantly renew the water in the pot and take away the salt. (And this is the fast way!)

In a bowl, beat the flour and egg with a pinch of pepper. Thin it out with just enough cold water to make a thick batter, about the same texture as pancake batter.

Pat the cod dry. Place the pieces in the batter and leave them there while you heat the sunflower oil.

Put enough oil in a large skillet to come about 2/3 up the sides of the pieces of cod. Heat the oil over medium-high heat, and fry the cod for 2 to 3 minutes total – just enough to turn the batter golden. (You do not need to cook the fish through at this point.) Drain on paper towels.

Heat the 1 Tbsp [15 mL] of olive oil over medium heat in a pot large enough to hold all the pieces of cod without touching. Reduce the heat to low and sauté the onions slowly until they are soft and golden, 15 to 20 minutes. Do not brown them.

Place the cod on the onions and add the tomato, garlic and parsley as well as pepper to taste. Cover and simmer for another 20 minutes.

Transfer the fish and sauce to a large platter and serve at the table.

Meat in general seems to appear on the Tuscan table
at times of celebration, and because of its rarity it becomes a real treat.

FOWL, MEAT AND WILD GAME

ROASTED GARLIC CHICKEN AND GRILLED VEGETABLES

Any time, anywhere, with any friends, this dish always comes up a winner. If I may borrow a phrase, it's finger-licking good. The grilled vegetables are cooked lightly for a nice firm texture.

INGREDIENTS

ROASTED GARLIC CHICKEN

1	whole roasting chicken (2–3 lbs [1–1.5 kg])
	salt
	freshly ground black pepper
	handful of fresh thyme
	OR 1 Tbsp [15 mL] dried thyme oil
4 cloves	garlic, skin on

GRILLED VEGETABLES

2 sprigs	thyme
	OR 1 tsp [5 mL] dried thyme
2 sprigs	rosemary
2 Tbsp [25 mL]	olive oil
1	medium eggplant
2	medium zucchinis
2	medium bell peppers, any colour
4	medium roma tomatoes
	salt
	freshly ground black pepper

SERVES 4

RECOMMENDED WINE
Chianti
RECOMMENDED PRODUCERS
Castello di Brolio, Castello di Gabbiano, Cecchi, Lilliano, Melini, Nozzole
Chianti is the ideal match for a menu that is simplicity itself.

PREPARATION

Preheat the oven to 350°F [180°C].

Wash the chicken well inside and out and dry it with paper towels. Lightly season the chicken inside with salt and pepper and stuff the chicken with thyme. Spread a bit of oil evenly over the skin of the chicken.

Put the chicken in a cast-iron pan with the unpeeled garlic cloves. Roast the bird for 45 minutes, basting it with the pan juices every 10 minutes or so.

While the chicken is roasting, prepare the vegetables. Rub the thyme and rosemary to release the aromas and add to the 2 Tbsp [30 mL] oil in a large bowl. Cut the eggplant and zucchinis into large strips and place them in the flavoured oil.

Bring a small pot of water to a boil. Cut the peppers in half lengthwise, remove the seeds and stems and boil the peppers for 2 minutes. Remove the peppers from the water and cut them in long strips. Add the peppers to the eggplant and zucchinis in the olive oil.

Slice the tomatoes 1/4 in. [5 mm] thick and add them to the other vegetables. Toss gently to cover everything with oil.

Preheat the barbecue or grill before the chicken is done.

When the chicken is nearly cooked, dry the vegetables with paper towels and grill them very quickly to keep them al dente, 2 to 3 minutes.

Once the chicken is thoroughly cooked, remove it from the oven and cut into 4 pieces. Place the vegetables in a warm serving dish. Season with salt and pepper to taste. Remove the skin from the garlic cloves. Arrange the chicken pieces and garlic on the vegetables and serve.

Pollo fritto di casa

HOME-FRIED CHICKEN

This chicken is already cooked before the batter goes on, so the deep frying just gives it a crispy coating. A crunchy salad with oil and vinegar dressing is an ideal partner.

INGREDIENTS

6	chicken thighs
3 cloves	garlic, crushed
1 tsp [5 mL]	minced fresh chili
1 Tbsp [15 mL]	paprika
	juice of 1 lemon
1 Tbsp [15 mL]	balsamic vinegar
	salt
	freshly ground black pepper
	oil for deep frying

BATTER

1 cup [250 mL]	all-purpose flour
1/2 cup [125 mL]	chickpea flour
1 Tbsp [15 mL]	baking powder
1 1/2 cups [375 mL]	cold water
	salt
	freshly ground black pepper
2	lemons, cut in wedges

SERVES 4 TO 6

PREPARATION

In a large bowl, season the chicken with garlic, chili, paprika, lemon juice, vinegar, salt and pepper. Mix well and let it marinate in the fridge for about 2 hours.

Preheat the oven to 375°F [190°C].

Prick each piece of chicken with the point of a knife to allow the flavour to penetrate. Place the chicken on baking racks and set the racks on rimmed baking sheets. Bake for 30 minutes, or until the juices run clear. Let the chicken cool.

In a large pot, heat the oil almost to the smoking point.

In a wide bowl, combine the flours, baking powder, water, salt and pepper and mix well. Dip the chicken thighs in the batter, coating them evenly, and deep-fry them until the batter is crisp and golden brown. Drain the chicken on paper towels, and serve with lemon wedges.

RECOMMENDED WINE
Chianti Classico
RECOMMENDED PRODUCERS
Castello di Fonterutoli, Castello di Volpaia, Fattoria di Felsina

What better wine to invoke the red-wine-with-white-meat mantra? Cherries, leather and earth make up the magic flavours of one of Italy's best-known reds.

TURKEY BREAST CUTLETS WITH PARMESAN CHEESE

These cutlets are the Tuscan version of schnitzel. They're made in every home, often as a quick lunch served with a salad, and maybe a spoonful of warm tomato sauce on top. Try a dollop of salsa di pomodoro on page 164 or fonduta di pomodoro on page 63.

INGREDIENTS

1 Tbsp [15 mL]	butter
1 cup [250 mL]	dry breadcrumbs
	freshly ground black pepper
5 oz [150 g]	Parmesan cheese, grated (about 2/3 cup [150 mL])
one 1 1/2 lb [750 g]	boneless breast of turkey
1	egg, lightly beaten
2 Tbsp [25 mL]	vegetable oil

SERVES 6

PREPARATION

Preheat the oven to 400°F [200°C]. Grease a baking dish with the butter.

Season the breadcrumbs with pepper and half of the Parmesan. No salt is needed because of the cheese.

Cut the turkey breast into 6 equal slices. Dip each slice in the egg, then in the breadcrumbs, being sure to coat both sides. Heat the oil in a skillet over medium heat and cook the turkey slices until they're golden brown, about 3 minutes per side.

Transfer the turkey to the prepared baking dish, cover with the remaining Parmesan and bake for 10 minutes or until the cheese is melted and bubbling and the turkey juices run clear. Serve immediately.

RECOMMENDED WINE
Chianti Colli Fiorentini
RECOMMENDED PRODUCERS
Baggiolino, Lilliano, Lucignano, Torre
a Decima
The hills of Florence are home to this
humble Chianti. Its medium-bodied flavours
of cherries, leather and earth and its
dry finish make this wine the ideal picnic
or lunchtime red.

HUNTING SEASON

Tuscans are passionate hunters. Often, in fact, autumn isn't even referred to by its name; it's just called hunting season. In September, those first gunshots ringing through the valleys signal that fall is here, with winter close behind. The marathon has begun. Fall is the busiest and most bountiful season of all, and a lot of activity is aimed at putting away supplies for the winter: there are mushrooms to dry, grapes to make into wine, tomatoes to make into sauces and bottle, and wild meat to preserve or freeze.

ONLY RARELY can you buy wild game in the market. Any game hunted is for private use only. That is one of the rules in Italy's game management system, which does a good job, I think, of balancing the needs of wildlife with the human desire to hunt.

Farmers are a big part of the equation. Wild animals roam freely through their farms, often feeding on part of their crops. Such a large percentage of the land is agricultural that the animals could not survive if they had to live only on public land. So the farmers leave them alone and the government pays restitution for any damage. Everybody's happy. The animals are well fed and undisturbed, and the farmers receive compensation for helping to keep them that way.

On some farms, all hunting is prohibited. These are the *riserve di caccia*, where wild game is protected even during hunting season, so the populations can maintain their numbers. Our 54 acres at Villa Delia, and many of the farms that surround us, make up a riserva di caccia. It's beautiful to see wild hare, pheasants, quails, wild ducks, boar and deer wandering about. I have to admit, though, it's an annoyance when they pull down the wires in the vineyard or trample crops or feed on the grapes. We're not allowed to bother them, but to keep them from bothering us, we do protect our gardens with high wire fences. And we might yell and jump up and down to shoo them away now and then.

Hunting season lasts from September through November, but the openings are very short and specific to a certain type of game. For three days you can go to one small area and hunt one kind of animal. Then that area is off limits and another one down the road opens up for two days. Hunters can follow the openings from place to place, but they don't stay long enough in one area to wipe out the animal populations. Fair game.

As a kid I remember being scared by all the noise of hunting season. The morning silence would be shattered by gunshots at about six or seven o'clock. Each shot would be accompanied by endless echoes – bang, b-bang, b-bang, bang, b-bang – it was a weird, almost continuous din for hours. Finally, when the church bells called everyone to Mass, it stopped. The bells brought peace on earth.

The passion for hunting is missing in me. I tried it a few times but I never became a hunter, although I do like the taste of wild meat. But still, this is my favourite season. There is so much bustle and activity. Friends meet more often to share their catch and tell their tall tales – how big that hare was, how long it took to track that boar. And it all ends up around a table, with laughter, friendship and a toast to life.

HERBED TURKEY AND POTATO CASSEROLE

Turkey is a prized fowl in Tuscany. When I was growing up, every farm had a few because at harvest time, friends and neighbours would work together to bring in the grapes or wheat or olives. Turkey was the ideal meat to serve to all those hungry people.

INGREDIENTS

2 lbs [1 kg]	turkey thighs
2 cloves	garlic
1	small fresh chili pepper
	small handful of fresh sage leaves
1 branch	rosemary for each turkey thigh
1/4 cup [50 mL]	extra virgin olive oil
1/2 cup [125 mL]	white vinegar
4 cups [1 L]	classic meat broth *(see page 159)* or chicken stock
6	medium potatoes, cut in large cubes
	salt
	freshly ground black pepper

SERVES 6

PREPARATION

Place turkey thighs skin side up in a nonreactive baking dish. Finely chop the garlic, chili pepper, sage and rosemary leaves together. Spread the mixture over the skin side of the turkey. Pour oil, then vinegar over the turkey. Marinate for 4 hours in refrigerator.

Preheat the oven to 200°F [95°C].

Bake the turkey in marinade for 1 hour, until turkey skin is crisp.

Boil the broth and add it to pan. Spread potatoes around the pan. Add salt and pepper to taste. Return to oven and cook for 30 minutes, until the potatoes are tender.

Arrange the potatoes on a warm platter. Slice the turkey thighs and serve with the pan juices.

BREAST OF DUCK RAPIDO

*We don't say quack quack, we say quick quick. Preparing duck doesn't have
to be involved and time consuming. This is a great dish for a family meal or for
entertaining. Serve it with pommes frites and a side salad.*

INGREDIENTS

4	medium duck breasts
4 cloves	garlic, cut in half
	salt
	freshly ground black pepper
2 Tbsp [30 mL]	olive oil
4 Tbsp [60 mL]	Dijon mustard
2	eggs, beaten
1 cup [250 mL]	breadcrumbs

SERVES 4

PREPARATION

Preheat the oven to 375°F [190°C].

Make a couple of small incisions on the skin side of each breast and insert the garlic into the meat. Salt and pepper the breasts to taste.

Heat the oil in a sauté pan over medium heat, and place the duck breasts in, skin side down. Fry them for 4 to 5 minutes per side, or until they're browned all over. Remove the duck breasts from the pan and dry them thoroughly with paper towels.

Brush the breasts on all sides with mustard. Have beaten eggs and breadcrumbs in separate flat bowls. Dip each breast first in egg then in the breadcrumbs.

Place the breasts skin side up in a baking dish and roast for about 20 minutes. The duck is done when the meat offers some resistance when pressed but still has some give to it.

RECOMMENDED WINE
Morellino di Scansano Riserva
RECOMMENDED PRODUCERS
Banti, Cecchi, Le Pupille, Motta, Moris Farms

The southwest corner of Tuscany, so close to the Mediterranean, produces this wonderful, soft, voluptuous red. You'll need the riserva to stand up to the duck.

ROASTED RABBIT

I like rabbit very much for two reasons. The first: my grandmother fried it and my mother roasted it with rosemary. I loved it either way. The second: Grandma and Mamma let me sell the rabbit skins in the market. I ate a lot of rabbits for six months while I saved for my first tennis shoes, a pair of blue Filas. This roasted rabbit goes nicely with broad noodles tossed in butter and cheese.

INGREDIENTS

3 Tbsp [45 mL]	extra virgin olive oil
2 cloves	garlic, coarsely chopped
1 branch	rosemary, coarsely chopped
	handful of sage, coarsely chopped
	salt
	freshly ground black pepper
one 2 lb [1 kg]	rabbit, cut in 6 pieces
3/4 cup [175 mL]	white wine
2 cups [500 mL]	classic meat broth *(see page 159)* or chicken stock, as needed

SERVES 6

PREPARATION

Combine the oil with the garlic, rosemary, sage, salt and pepper. Toss the rabbit pieces with the mixture and refrigerate for 1 hour.

Preheat the oven to 350°F [180°C].

In an unoiled ovenproof pot, brown the rabbit over medium heat for 4 to 5 minutes. When the rabbit picks up a bit of colour, pour in the wine. Simmer until all the wine has evaporated.

Transfer the pot to the oven. Pour in 1 cup of the broth and roast the rabbit for 40 minutes. Move the pieces around with a wooden spoon occasionally to prevent sticking. If the meat appears to be drying out, add more of the broth.

When the rabbit is tender, serve it with any pan juices poured on top.

RECOMMENDED WINE
Morellino di Scansano
RECOMMENDED PRODUCERS
Banti, Cecchi, Le Pupille, Motta, Moris Farms

Morellino, a Sangiovese clone, is a rising star in southern Tuscany. The climate is cool-coastal, but the flavours of the wine mirror those of the roasted rabbit – warm, robust and long.

VEAL BUNDLES WITH AROMATIC GARDEN FLAVOURS

These were a big hit when I demonstrated them at New York's well-known cooking school La Cucina Italiana.

INGREDIENTS

8	medium prawns, shelled and deveined
3 Tbsp [50 mL]	olive oil
1/2 cup [125 mL]	shaved fresh fennel
8	scallops of veal, pounded thin
	salt
	freshly ground black pepper
8	sundried tomatoes
	zest of 2 lemons
1/4 cup [60 mL]	chopped parsley
	flour for dredging
2 Tbsp [30 mL]	butter
1/2 cup [125 mL]	dry white wine
2 cups [500 mL]	veal stock

SERVES 4

PREPARATION

Sauté the prawns in 1 Tbsp [15 mL] of the olive oil for 1 minute per side. Set aside.

To the same pan, add another 1 Tbsp [15 mL] of olive oil and the fennel, and cook over medium heat until browned and soft, approximately 5 minutes. Set aside.

Lay veal scallops on a flat surface and salt and pepper both sides. Place 1 prawn and 1 sundried tomato in the centre of each veal slice, and add a spoonful of fennel, a pinch of lemon zest and a pinch of parsley. (Reserve some parsley for garnish.) Roll the veal slice over the filling, tuck in the ends and continue rolling to make a neat package.

Spread flour on a board or plate and dust each roll with flour on each side, shaking off the excess.

Heat 1/2 the butter and 1 Tbsp [15 mL] of the oil in a skillet over medium-high heat. Brown the veal bundles on all sides for a total of 2 to 3 minutes. Remove the bundles to a heated plate and keep warm.

Increase the heat and add the wine to the skillet, shaking it to distribute the liquid until the alcohol evaporates. Add the veal stock, the remaining 1 Tbsp [15 mL] of the butter and the remaining parsley and cook for 2 minutes more.
Pour the sauce over the veal bundles and serve.

RECOMMENDED WINE
Chardonnay
RECOMMENDED PRODUCERS
Castellare di Castellina (Canonico), Ruffino Libaio, San Felice (Capitolare del Muschio), Terrabianca (Piano della Capella), Tua Rita (Sileno)

Tuscan Chardonnay is richer than its northern Italian counterparts yet its style is light, vibrant and fresh. It will stand up to the veal without overpowering the seafood.

La Maremma

Until recent times, this southernmost region of Tuscany was considered a rural backwater of farms, ranches and fishing villages. Not anymore. Maremma is still the market basket of Tuscany, providing a great percentage of its meat, produce and fish, but now travellers have discovered its beauty.

THE GORGEOUS COASTLINE rewards them with sandy beaches and views of Isola d'Elba, Il Giglio, Capraia and, on a clear day, the beautiful peaks of Corsica. Visitors seek out the hidden fishing villages, built on cliffs and in tiny coves for protection from successive waterborne enemies over the centuries.

Inland from the coastline is the flat farming country, reclaimed in this century from marshland. With its moist soil, clean maritime air and well-timed rains, this land can grow anything. Throughout Tuscany, markets sell tomatoes, fennel, artichokes and other vegetables grown in Maremma.

As the land slopes up gradually from the sea, you see more cattle, sheep and goats. The cowboys, *butteri*, work here. Some of them are probably distant relatives of the butteri who emigrated to North America two centuries ago to contribute their skills to the ranches of the New World and become the original Western cowhands, according to the stories in this part of the world.

The low hills lead to the mountains and high plateau, where vineyards and olive groves grow. In the northern part of Maremma are the villages that make Morellino di Scansano, a red wine that has become extremely sought-after. Like the famous Brunello di Montalcino, which grows in the neighbouring Siena district, this is a deep, hearty wine made entirely of Sangiovese grapes.

Throughout the region, wild game thrives. Duck was once a staple food when the land was swampy, and since reclamation, wild boars and hares have become abundant. Many of the game recipes that have become popular in Tuscany originated here.

The first people to recognize the potential of this land were the Etruscans. Maremma was the centre of their territory, a group of city-states and agrarian areas whose military power lasted from the eighth century BC to 280 BC when Rome conquered them. Today, when you visit a small village in Maremma, you will probably find some proud display of its Etruscan heritage.

After the Roman defeat, the Etruscan civilization waned. The aqueducts and embankments crumbled, allowing the rivers and sea to invade the land. The name Maremma, comes either from the Italian *marittima*, meaning from the sea, and *memma*, marshy soil, or from the Spanish *marismas* or marsh. Once the coastal land became marshy, the area was almost deserted for a long time. As a consequence, it is now one of the most un-touched, natural areas in Tuscany.

I go there about twice a year, and every time I travel through, Maremma looks more beautiful. You can stay at a lovely inn, a working farm or one of the many campsites, and you will find yourself far away from the bustle of Florence or Pisa. This is the most rural district of Tuscany, where you will mark the time by nothing more than the breeze from the sea and the sun's reflection off the fields.

If you travel from Florence to Rome, follow in the footsteps of the Romans along the coastline, and occasionally veer inland in their tracks. (Who are we to disagree with the Romans?) Enjoy the scenic drive and the salty winds from the Mediterranean before you reach the Eternal City. The Romans knew what they were doing. And they learned much of it from the Etruscans, for whom this good land was home.

ROLLED BREAST OF VEAL

At weddings, first communions or christenings, you're likely to see this festive dish. Veal is a luxury, so it's stretched with a delicious filling. The breast is the least expensive and most flavourful cut of veal, but get the butcher to bone and trim it for you because it's a time-consuming job. Serve this dish with potatoes roasted with rosemary and sage, and spinach sautéed with garlic, lemon juice and nutmeg.

INGREDIENTS

1/4 cup [50 mL]	olive oil
1/4 cup [50 mL]	diced eggplant
4 cloves	garlic, finely chopped
1/2	medium onion, diced
1/3 cup [75 mL]	fresh shelled peas
1/4 lb [125 g]	cooked ham, cut in small dice
6–7	sage leaves
1/4 lb [125 g]	freshly grated Parmesan cheese (about 1 1/2 cups [375 mL])
1	egg
2 Tbsp [25 mL]	pistachios
2 sprigs	lemon thyme, finely chopped
	salt
	freshly ground black pepper
one 1 1/4-lb [625-g]	boned breast of veal
	juice of 1 lemon
1/2 cup [125 mL]	classic meat broth *(see page 159)* or chicken stock

SERVES 4 TO 6

PREPARATION

Heat 2 Tbsp [25 mL] of the oil in a skillet over medium heat. Sauté the eggplant, garlic and onion until the eggplant is soft, about 5 minutes. Set aside to cool.

Bring a small pot of water to a boil and blanch the peas until they turn bright green. Drain them immediately and put them in cold water to stop the cooking. Drain the peas again when they're cool.

Preheat the oven to 400°F [200°C].

In a bowl, combine the ham, sage, Parmesan, egg, pistachios, thyme and the eggplant mixture. Season with salt and pepper, mix well, then gently stir in the peas.

Rub the veal with the remaining 2 Tbsp [25 mL] of the oil. Sprinkle it with salt and pepper and place it in a roasting pan. Spread the filling over the veal. Roll up the meat tightly in jelly-roll fashion. Secure it with string. Pour the lemon juice and broth over the meat and roast it for 1 hour, or until it is tender when pricked with a fork.

Remove the roast from the oven and let it rest at least 5 minutes before slicing.

RECOMMENDED WINE
Chianti Classico
RECOMMENDED PRODUCERS
Castello di Fonterutoli, Castello di Volpaia, Fattoria di Felsina

Chianti Classico, between Florence and Siena, is the heart of the Chianti region and home to the richest and most full-bodied Chiantis.

MEDALLIONS OF VEAL WITH LEMON CAPER SAUCE

Quick, easy and elegant, these veal medallions need nothing more than your favourite steamed vegetables and some roasted new potatoes.

INGREDIENTS

8	medallions of veal tenderloin, cut 1 1/2 in. [4 cm] thick
	salt
	freshly ground pepper
	flour for dredging
	olive oil for frying
2 Tbsp [30 mL]	white wine
	juice of 1/2 lemon
1 cup [250 mL]	chicken stock
1/2 tsp [2 mL]	capers

SERVES 4

PREPARATION

Season the medallions with salt and pepper and dust with flour on both sides.

Drizzle just enough olive oil into a large skillet to cover the bottom, and heat over medium heat. Place the veal in the pan and sear each side for 2 to 3 minutes. Remove the veal from the pan, set aside and keep warm.

Still over medium heat, deglaze the pan with the white wine and add the lemon juice. Add the chicken stock and the capers and simmer for 3 to 4 minutes.

Return the veal to the pan and continue to simmer for another 3 to 4 minutes, or until the veal is cooked to medium. Remove the veal and place it on a warmed serving platter.

Further reduce the sauce to a thick consistency, if necessary. Pour the sauce over the veal and serve.

RECOMMENDED WINE
Pomino Bianco
RECOMMENDED PRODUCER
Frescobaldi

Frescobaldi's Pomino Il Benefizio is a mouth-watering Chardonnay and a wonderful foil for veal.

VEAL AND ZUCCHINI PIE

This Luccan specialty is a quick and easy dish to make for a dinner party. Once it's in the oven, you can spend time with your guests. Serve it with a crisp salad and you have a nice light meal.

INGREDIENTS

1 Tbsp [15 mL]	butter
2 Tbsp [25 mL]	flour
1 cup [250 mL]	milk, hot
	salt
	pinch of nutmeg
2 Tbsp [25 mL]	butter
6	medium zucchinis, thinly sliced
	salt
	freshly ground black pepper
4 Tbsp [60 mL]	grated Parmesan cheese
12 thin slices	raw veal, 6–8 in. [15–20 cm] in diameter
4	medium ripe tomatoes, sliced
1/4 cup [50 mL]	whipping cream

SERVES 6

PREPARATION

Preheat the oven to 375°F [190°C].

Prepare a white sauce: melt the 1 Tbsp [15 mL] butter in a small pot over medium heat. Whisk in the flour and continue to whisk for 2 to 3 minutes until it lightens in colour. Add 1/4 of the milk at a time, and whisk continuously until the sauce thickens. Remove the sauce from the heat and stir in the salt and nutmeg.

To assemble the pie, use the 2 Tbsp [25 mL] butter to grease a 9 x 13 in. [23 x 32 cm] dish. Arrange 1/4 of the zucchini slices in a layer on the bottom, and season with salt and pepper. Spread 1/4 of the white sauce over top, then sprinkle on 1/4 of the Parmesan. Place 4 slices of veal on top.

Repeat for two more layers. For the top layer, start with the zucchini, then tomatoes, salt and pepper, white sauce and Parmesan.

Bake the pie for 45 minutes, or until the top is golden and bubbling. If the top looks too dry, moisten it with a little whipping cream.

Let the pie rest for 5 to 10 minutes before serving. Cut the pie into wedges or small squares to serve.

RECOMMENDED WINE
Chianti
RECOMMENDED PRODUCERS
Antinori, Cecchi, Frescobaldi, Melini, Ruffino

A simple, straight-ahead Chianti matches the simplicity of the dish and does a fine job of cutting through the melted cheese too.

TUSCAN OSSO BUCO

*In Tuscany we make osso buco with more sauce than the classic Milanese way.
It is at its best when served with a risotto, which will catch the sauce.*

INGREDIENTS

4	veal shank slices, at least 2 fingers thick
	salt
	freshly ground black pepper
	flour for dredging
4 Tbsp [60 mL]	vegetable oil
1	medium onion
1	carrot
1 stalk	celery, with leaves
2 cloves	garlic
1 cup [250 mL]	canned tomatoes with juice
	handful of Italian parsley
	handful of fresh sage leaves
1 small branch	rosemary
2 cups [500 mL]	dry white wine
1 cup [250 mL]	classic meat broth *(see page 159)*

GREMOLATA

2 tsp [10 mL]	grated lemon zest
1 clove	garlic, minced
4 tsp [20 mL]	finely chopped Italian parsley

SERVES 4

PREPARATION

Preheat oven to 400°F [200°C].

Season shanks with salt and pepper, then dredge in flour, shaking off any excess.

Heat oil in a sauté pan over high heat. Sear the veal shanks until golden brown all over. Place seared shanks in a roasting pan large enough to hold them in one layer.

Coarsely chop the onion, carrot, celery and garlic together, and add them to the roasting pan. Coarsely chop the tomatoes and add them, along with the herbs, wine and broth. Season with salt and pepper.

Cook the veal uncovered in the oven for 45 minutes, until the tops of the shanks start to appear crisp. The liquid should be just bubbling, not boiling furiously. Turn the shanks over after 45 minutes and cook for another 15 minutes, until the liquid is reduced to a thick and creamy consistency. The meat is done when it is tender when pierced with a knife.

GREMOLATA
To make the gremolata, combine the lemon zest, garlic and parsley in a small bowl.

Serve one veal shank per person with sauce and a sprinkling of gremolata.

RECOMMENDED WINE
Rosso di Montalcino
RECOMMENDED PRODUCERS
Castello Banfi, Barbi, Il Poggione, Val di Suga

Rossi di Montalcino is the kinder, gentler, less expensive version of Brunello. This is a fruit-driven, gutsy red made from Sangiovese.

Bracioline rustiche

COUNTRY-STYLE PORK CHOPS

Pork is reasonably priced and delicious, and it is probably the most popular meat in Tuscany. We use every part of the pig, and have dozens of ways to cook all of them. These pork chops benefit from the walnut overtones of the Parmesan cheese.

INGREDIENTS

4 Tbsp [60 mL]	olive oil
2 cloves	garlic
4	pork rib chops, 6–8 oz [175–250 g] each
	salt
2/3 cup [150 mL]	freshly grated Parmesan cheese

SERVES 4 TO 6

PREPARATION

In a skillet, heat the oil over medium heat. Sauté the whole garlic cloves until they just turn golden, then remove them from the pan.

Increase the heat to high and brown the pork chops on both sides. Searing them this way will create a crust and help them to retain moisture so they don't dry out during cooking. Reduce the heat to medium and cook the chops until they are done to your preference, 4 to 6 minutes in total.

Sprinkle the chops with salt and top them evenly with the Parmesan. Cover the pan, and cook over medium-low heat until the cheese has melted. Serve immediately.

RECOMMENDED WINE
Chianti Classico
RECOMMENDED PRODUCERS
Badia Coltibuono, Castello di Verrazzano, Ricasoli, San Felice

The richest and most full-bodied Chiantis are Chianti Classico. The intense fruit of these well-crafted reds gives the rich meat and cheese a run for its money.

ROAST PORK WITH CARDOONS

Every Tuscan garden has a couple of large silver cardoon plants. The plants are beautiful, and the stalks of this relative of the artichoke make a delicious winter vegetable. They are little known in North America, but I have found them in Chinese vegetable markets. They look like giant silvery-grey celery stalks. If you can't find cardoons, a scalloped potato dish with tomatoes accompanies this pork well.

INGREDIENTS

one 4 lb [2 kg]	loin roast of pork , rolled and tied
	salt
	freshly ground black pepper
4	sage leaves, finely chopped
4 sprigs	rosemary, finely chopped
4 Tbsp [60 mL]	olive oil
1 cup [250 mL]	Vin Santo or other sweet white wine
1	small carrot, finely chopped
1	small onion, finely chopped
2 cloves	garlic, crushed
1 tsp [5 mL]	cayenne pepper
1 cup [250 mL]	classic meat broth *(see page 159)*
	or chicken stock

CARDOONS

2 lbs [1 kg]	cardoons
1 Tbsp [15 mL]	lemon juice
1 lb [500 g]	tomatoes, peeled, seeded, drained
	and finely chopped
2 Tbsp [30 mL]	chopped prosciutto
1 Tbsp [15 mL]	olive oil
	salt
	freshly ground black pepper

SERVES 8

PREPARATION

Preheat the oven to 375°F [190°C].

Rub the pork roast with salt, pepper, sage and rosemary.

Heat the olive oil in a large ovenproof pot over high heat. Brown the roast all over, then add the wine and continue cooking until the alcohol evaporates.

Add the carrot, onion, garlic, cayenne and broth, and put the pot in the oven, uncovered, to cook for 45 minutes. Check it periodically and if the liquid disappears during cooking, add 1 cup [250 mL] of warm water.

Reduce the heat to 350°F [180°C], cover and cook for another 45 minutes.

RECOMMENDED WINE
Vino Nobile di Montepulciano
RECOMMENDED PRODUCERS
Avignonesi, Il Conventino, Fassati, Poderi Boscarelli, Poliziano, Romeo, Valdipiatta Vino Nobile has been described as a cross between the elegant Chianti Classico and the powerful Brunello di Montalcino.

Remove the lid and cook uncovered for a final 10 minutes. The pork should be nice and tender, and when you pierce it with a fork, clear juices should come out. If the juices are still red, cook the meat a bit longer.

Prepare the cardoons by removing the tough outer ribs. Cut the inner stalks into 2 in. [5 cm] pieces and drop them in acidulated water as you go, to prevent discoloration.

Add salt and lemon juice to a pot of water and bring it to a boil. Put the cardoons in the pot, return the water to a boil, then reduce the heat and simmer for 1 1/2 hours until the cardoons are tender. Drain them and return them to the pot.

Add the tomatoes, prosciutto and 1 Tbsp [15 mL] of oil. Cook gently for about 35 minutes, or until the tomatoes are soft. Season to taste with salt and pepper.

Serve the cardoons with slices of pork.

CHIANTI

I often find myself explaining the geography of the regions of Tuscany – and of one in particular. Chianti, or better, the wine country, is a district of Tuscany, not a separate province as so many visitors think. In fact, Tuscans consider Chianti the most traditional and characteristic region in all of Tuscany, and its people are the most intent on protecting their heritage.

MUCH OF THE WINE-GROWING region called Chianti lies between the historic cities of Florence and Siena, which overran it in turn as they attempted to conquer each other over the centuries. With all that conquering back and forth, the two cities today are hard to tell apart. The Chianti region reflects them both in landscape and in architecture.

One part of Chianti, Chianti Classico, was particularly prized by both cities. Legend says that Florence and Siena finally decided the borders of Chianti Classico by sending out a rooster from each city to walk as far as it could in a day. The place where each rooster stopped walking would determine the limit of that city's territory. Naturally, each city wanted its bird to travel as far as possible into the best wine-growing land. The Sienese fed their rooster well so it would be strong and tireless. The Florentines starved theirs so it would be hungry and searching for food. The Florentine strategy won, and their ravenous rooster claimed a larger chunk of the wine-producing area. Everything in between is now Chianti Classico, the best of the seven Chianti appellations.

There is a phrase, *i dolci uomini del Chianti*, the sweet men of Chianti. I find the men of the area articulate and aristocratic. Their deep sense of belonging gives them a peaceful look and gentlemanly way. The women are beautiful – full of life and sweetness, with a harmonious, musical way of moving. And the playful children with their lustrous, probing eyes, can look straight into your heart.

Timeless Chianti may be the region of Tuscany where you find the most complete package of history, culture, food, wine and people. I have many friends in this region and I will be visiting them throughout this book. So let's travel the Chianti road together, and *buon viaggio*.

My Super Tuscan friend,
il Marchese Piero Antinori.

THE WINES OF CHIANTI

Centuries before the DOC *(Denomina-zione di origine controllata)* was instituted to regulate wine production in Italy, Chianti organized itself into seven zones: *Chianti Classico, Chianti Colli Aretini, Chianti Colli Fiorentini, Chianti Colli Pisani, Chianti Colli Senesi, Chianti Montalbano* and *Chianti Rufina.*

Traditionally the wine comes in two styles. Chianti, the fresh, fruity wine, which used to be bottled in the characteristic straw-encased round bottle *(fiasco),* is meant to be enjoyed young. The drier Chianti Riserva is richer, and meant for a bit of aging.

From the 1870s on, a Chianti had to be made to a formula: a blend of Sangiovese and Canaiolo, with small amounts of the white grapes Trebbiano and Malvasia. The formula changed over the years as producers preferred to use less and less white grape content. Today, some of the finest wines of Chianti can no longer be called Chianti; their producers have eliminated the white grapes and added non-traditional grapes such as Cabernet Sauvignon or Merlot. These new wines have earned the nickname SuperTuscans, an unofficial, unrecognized category inspired by Antinori's Sassicaia. The DOC is starting to come up with ways of recognizing them, but many of these new blends still receive the humble designation, *vino da tavola,* table wine. Pay no attention; they're some of the best wines coming out of Italy today.

ROAST SUCKLING PIG

You need a brick oven, 35 guests and an accordion player if you're going to roast a suckling pig. If you can fulfill those requirements, this is an easy and spectacular way to entertain. Invite half friends and half enemies, and you'll have more friends at the end. It's great with roast potatoes, boiled corn on the cob, a hearty salad and lots of red wine. E viva la vita!

INGREDIENTS

one 35 lb [16 kg]	suckling pig, cleaned
12 cloves	garlic
6	large onions, coarsely chopped
6	medium tart apples, peeled and coarsely chopped
2 handfuls	sage leaves
2 loaves	day-old baguette, roughly chopped, soaked in milk and squeezed dry
	coarsely crushed black pepper
	coarse salt
1 cup [250 mL]	olive oil

SERVES 35
(WITH LOTS OF CRACKLING)

RECOMMENDED WINE
Vino Nobile di Montepulciano
RECOMMENDED PRODUCERS
Avignonesi, Il Conventino, Fassati, Poderi Boscarelli, Poliziano, Romeo, Valdipiatta
Vino Nobile is an ideal accompaniment to pork. It is substantial in the mouth but not overpoweringly tannic or dry.

PREPARATION

Preheat the oven to 450°F [230°C]. If you don't have a roasting pan large enough for the pig, connect several roasting pans with foil to catch the drippings, and place a rack on top of the pans. If the drippings land on the floor of the oven, they will burn and impart a bitter taste to the meat.

Dry the pig thoroughly, inside and out, with paper towels. Cut 6 cloves of the garlic in half lengthwise. Make incisions through the skin of the pig in a dozen places, and insert a piece of garlic into each. The garlic flavours the meat, and the cuts allow steam to escape during roasting so the skin becomes nice and crispy.

Place the onions, apples, sage leaves and the remaining 6 cloves of garlic in a food processor, and process until everything is finely chopped. Add this mixture to the bread. Stir in 1 Tbsp [15 mL] each of salt and pepper. Add enough olive oil to make a thick paste.

Coat the inside of the pig with the onion and apple paste. Close the cavity with skewers. Rub the outside of the pig first with olive oil, then with a generous amount of salt and pepper. Place the pig on a rack and cover with foil. Roast it 1 1/2 hours for every 10 lbs [4 1/2 kg]. In the last hour of roasting, remove the foil and reduce the heat to 375°F [190°C].

Remove the pig from the oven and allow it to stand for 15 minutes before carving (so everyone can admire it). Present it with the head on and an apple in its mouth, and tell your assembled friends that this is the way you like to serve apples.

To carve, use a cleaver and chop the pig crosswise into large chunks, then chop it lengthwise. Everyone will get meaty bones to eat with their hands – this is definitely for an outdoor party. If there's any left over, you are truly blessed, because there is no better meat for sandwiches.

NOT JUST MIXED BOILED MEATS

Bollito misto and soccer – two of the very few things that all Italians can agree on. This tender meat with its savoury broth is a favourite Sunday dinner everywhere in the country, and it varies little from region to region. It is accompanied by the piquant salsa verde, boiled potatoes and simply prepared carrots or leeks. Happy Sunday.

INGREDIENTS

4	large carrots, peeled, coarsely chopped
3 large stalks	celery, trimmed and coarsely chopped
4	small onions, peeled, coarsely chopped
1	medium beef tongue, skinned and cleaned
1	calf's foot, approximately 1 lb [500 g]
1 lb [500 g]	beef brisket
one 2 lb [1 kg]	chicken
1 lb [500 g]	veal top round
1 lb [500 g]	beef shank
1 lb [500 g]	cotechino sausage
1 Tbsp [15 mL]	salt
1 Tbsp [15 mL]	cracked black pepper

SALSA VERDE

5	anchovy fillets
1/2 cup [125 mL]	breadcrumbs
1/4 cup [50 mL]	bollito misto broth or stock
4 cloves	garlic
2 Tbsp [25 mL]	capers
2	eggs, hard cooked
2 Tbsp [25 mL]	chopped parsley
	pinch of cayenne pepper
	juice of 1 lemon
1 cup [250 mL]	extra virgin olive oil

SERVES 8

PREPARATION

Half-fill a large stockpot with water and bring it to a boil. Add the vegetables, tongue and calf's foot, and return the water to a boil. Skim any froth from the surface and continue to do so as the dish cooks.

Add the brisket, cover, and reduce the heat so the liquid stays at a low boil for 40 minutes. Add the chicken, veal and beef shank, cover, and cook at a low boil for 1 hour.

Add the cotechino sausage, cover, and cook at a low boil for 1 hour more. Add the salt and pepper about 1/2 hour into this last phase. When it's finished cooking, the meat should be coming off the bones. Let the meat sit in the broth for 10 minutes before removing it to serve.

RECOMMENDED WINE
Brunello di Montalcino
RECOMMENDED PRODUCERS
Castello Banfi, Barbi, Biondi-Santi, Frescobaldi, Col d'Orcia

To serve, cut the chicken into 8 pieces, slice the cotechino, carve the remaining meats and transfer all the meat and chicken to a heated platter. Pour a little broth over top, and finish with a few grindings of pepper. Pass the salsa verde in a separate bowl.

SALSA VERDE
While the meat is cooking, put the anchovies, breadcrumbs, broth, garlic, capers, eggs, parsley, cayenne and lemon juice in the blender and purée to a thick sauce. With the blender still running, add the oil in a thin stream. Taste and adjust the seasonings, and it is ready to serve.

Expect the sweetness of the gently cooked meat to complement the leaner structure of this magnificent, complex red.

TRATTORIA STEW

If you can find an authentic local truckstop or cafe, you'll find good food at a reasonable price. That's as true in Tuscany as it is in North America. This hearty one-course meal is a favourite at such places. It's best served on a bed of egg noodles, plain rice or mashed potatoes.

INGREDIENTS

1 lb [500 g]	braising beef, veal, pork or venison
1 Tbsp [15 mL]	butter
1	medium carrot, finely diced
1	large onion, finely diced
4 cloves	garlic, crushed
2 Tbsp [25 mL]	olive oil
4	medium ripe tomatoes, diced
1 sprig	marjoram
1 sprig	thyme
1 Tbsp [15 mL]	red wine vinegar
1/2 cup [125 mL]	beef stock or water
	salt
	crushed black pepper
1 Tbsp [15 mL]	tomato paste

SERVES 4

PREPARATION

Cut the meat into bite-sized cubes. Melt the butter over medium heat and sauté the carrot, onion and garlic for about 2 minutes, or until soft and lightly coloured.

Push the vegetables to one side of the pan and fry the meat until it is evenly browned. Add the oil, tomatoes, marjoram, thyme, vinegar, stock, salt and pepper and bring to a boil. Reduce the heat and simmer covered for about 30 minutes.

Add the tomato paste and cook 5 minutes longer, or until the meat is tender.

RECOMMENDED WINE
Chianti Colli Senesi
RECOMMENDED PRODUCERS
Chigi Saracini, Il Poggiolo

Chianti Colli Senesi comprises three main regions around Montalcino, Montepulciano and San Gimignano. The Sangiovese here can be quite refined, but usually is best for quaffing at lunchtime with a hearty trattoria stew.

FLORENTINE LIVER KEBABS

I first tasted these juicy, crunchy kebabs when I was eight. I had never willingly eaten liver before – but I liked this! One day soon, I'm going to make it for my son in the hopes that he will start to eat liver the same way I did. These kebabs go well with a salad or slices of summer-ripe tomato.

INGREDIENTS

2 cloves	garlic, finely chopped
1 Tbsp [15 mL]	fennel seed
2 Tbsp [35 mL]	extra virgin olive oil
1 1/2 lbs [750 g]	calf liver, cut into twelve 1 in. [2.5 cm] cubes
	salt
	freshly ground black pepper
	flour for dusting
2	eggs, beaten
1 cup [250 mL]	fine fresh breadcrumbs
6 cubes	stale bread, cut 1 in. [2.5 cm]
6	fresh bay leaves
1	lemon, quartered

SERVES 3

PREPARATION

Preheat the broiler to medium and place the rack 8 in. [20 cm] from the heat.

In a mortar, pound the garlic and fennel seed with the oil. Rub the cubes of liver with the mixture and season with salt and pepper. Dust them with flour, and dip them first in the beaten eggs and then in the breadcrumbs. Pat the breadcrumbs on to make sure they stick.

Arrange 4 cubes of liver with 2 cubes of bread and 2 bay leaves on each of 3 wooden skewers. Place the skewers under the broiler and cook for about 10 minutes, turning frequently to make sure the breadcrumbs don't burn. Adjust the heat, if necessary. They should come out medium-rare.

Arrange the kebabs on a platter with wedges of lemon.

RECOMMENDED WINE
Chianti Classico
RECOMMENDED PRODUCERS
Castello di Fonterutoli, Castello di Volpaia, Fattoria di Felsina

Truffles, cherries, leather and earth make up the magic flavours of one of Italy's best-known reds.

FLORENTINE TRIPE

Once a week the butcher would prepare tripe and offer it for sale, and he always sold out. Either honeycomb or smooth tripe will work with this recipe. Serve it as an antipasto, or accompany it with mashed potatoes for a main dish. You might want to prepare it the day before you plan to serve it, because tripe is one of those foods that taste better the next day.

INGREDIENTS

1 lb [500 g]	tripe, cut in 2 x 1 in. [5 x 2.5 cm] strips
2 cups [500 mL]	fonduta di pomodoro *(see page 63)* or other simple tomato sauce
1 sprig	marjoram
3	bay leaves
	salt
	freshly ground black pepper
1 cup [250 mL]	classic meat broth *(see page 159)* or chicken stock, as needed
4 Tbsp [60 mL]	Parmesan cheese

SERVES 4

PREPARATION

Place the strips of tripe in a large pan and cover with water. Bring the water to a boil, then reduce the heat and gently simmer, uncovered, for about 30 minutes, or until all the water evaporates.

Add the tomato sauce, marjoram and bay leaves; cover and simmer for 1 hour. (Be careful not to boil the sauce. Overcooking will make tripe tough, and then it's impossible to bring it back to tenderness.)

Taste for seasonings and texture. The tripe should be slightly firm and pleasant to the mouth, but not rubbery. Adjust the seasonings and, if the tripe had not yet reached the desired texture, gently simmer it, covered, for another 10 minutes. If the sauce is starting to cook away, add some broth.

When the tripe is done, sprinkle it with Parmesan, then serve.

RECOMMENDED WINE
Rosso di Montalcino
RECOMMENDED PRODUCERS
Castello Banfi, Barbi, Il Poggione, Val di Suga

The kinder, gentler, less expensive version of Brunello is a fruit-driven, gutsy red made from Sangiovese, the perfect match for this classic Tuscan dish.

FLORENTINE BEEFSTEAK

Florence is famous for this dish, and yet the preparation is so very simple. What's the secret? It's the special breed the meat comes from: Chianina beef. These animals were introduced by the Romans and they've been raised in the Val di Chiana ever since. To come close to the real Florentine experience, the meat you use should be a very thick porterhouse that's aged at least 21 days. Your butcher will be able to age it properly and cut it for you.

INGREDIENTS

one 34 oz [1.1 kg]	porterhouse steak, cut 1 1/2–2 inches [4–5 cm] thick
	salt
	freshly ground black pepper
4 Tbsp [60 mL]	olive oil
4 cloves	garlic, halved
1 branch	rosemary
1	lemon
	chopped parsley for garnish
1 tsp [5 mL]	extra virgin olive oil for garnish

SERVES 4

RECOMMENDED WINE
Chianti Classico
RECOMMENDED PRODUCERS
Badia Coltibuono, Castello di Verrazzano, Ricasoli, San Felice
The intense fruit of these well-crafted reds cuts deep into the fat and tannins of the beef.

PREPARATION

Trim the meat of all the fat around the outside. Season both sides of the steak with salt and pepper, and coat both sides with some of the oil. Pour the remaining oil into a dish. Add 1/2 the garlic and place the steak on top of it. Sprinkle the remaining garlic over the steak and lay the rosemary branch on top. Cover the steak and refrigerate it for 1 hour.

After 1 hour, remove the meat from the fridge and let it stand for 1 more hour at room temperature. (Don't worry about the health inspector.)

Preheat the broiler or barbecue to very hot. Before you cook the steak, remove all of the garlic and rosemary, otherwise they will burn and add bitterness to the dish. Leave the oil in the dish and keep the rosemary branch to use as a brush for the oil.

Grill or broil the first side about 10 minutes, until it is nice and crispy. Then turn the steak over and grill for about 3 minutes, or until it is cooked to your preference. Using the rosemary branch, brush the garlicky oil on the cooked side so it won't dry out.

When the steak is done, remove it from the grill and put it back in the dish with the remaining oil. Let it rest for 3 to 4 minutes, keeping it warm.

Just before serving, squeeze the juice of 1/2 lemon over the steak. Separate the meat from the bones and cut it on the diagonal into 1/2–3/4 in. [1–2 cm] slices.

To serve, stand the bone up in the middle of the serving platter and surround it with beef slices. Squeeze on the juice of the other 1/2 lemon, sprinkle with parsley and drizzle the extra virgin olive oil over top.

FLORENCE

On la mia toscana journey, I must stop a little longer in Florence because it's the hub. I'd like to tell you something about the culinary history of this blessed land, which started in this city, mostly with the Medici family around the late fourteenth century.

AT THE TIME, people didn't know Tuscany; they knew the Medicis, the aristocratic family that told the world about silk and art and war, and established Florence as the cultural heart of Europe. Florence was Italy in the same way London was England or Paris was France. The Medicis and other noble families entertained with extravagant banquets, which sometimes featured one hundred different dishes. Maybe these were expressions of wealth and display, or maybe the nobles were contributing to gastronomy in the same way they commissioned art or supported scientific research.

Over 600 years, the Florentines ruled all the other Tuscan cities at one time or other, and they implemented their style of politics, art and cuisine. They enriched the other regions, and vice versa. That is why we find a similar approach to food throughout Tuscany. Variations result from what grows best in each region because of climate or geography, rather than from any differences in philosophy.

The complicated cuisine of the Renaissance was contrary to the simple style for which Tuscany, and particularly Florence, is known now. Elaborate sauces have been replaced by a thread of extra virgin olive oil and some wild herbs. Today the Florentines say *meno è meglio*, less is more. But the genuine love of good food remains. Eating is as much an art as sculpture and architecture.

Florence is a haven for food exploration, with restaurants of every level. If you want waiters with white gloves, you will pay more, but the food may be just as good in a little local hole-in-the-wall. Eating in Florence is truly an experience, especially if you stay away from the restaurants with their menus posted out front in German, French and English. These places are trying to please tourists by catering to their tastes, and while the food might be fine, it won't be authentic.

For fun and adventure, get lost; meet people. Away from the main visitor trails you'll find little restaurants where the nearby storekeepers and workers eat. Most Tuscan produce ends up in Florence, and the daily menus will reflect the bounty of the market that day – tripe, fava beans, fennel – whatever is fresh and in season. That's when you're in for real Florentine food. One of my favourites is Le Fonticine Ristorante, right across the street from the Via Nazionale market, where the owner grills a superb *bistecca alla fiorentina*.

Florence offers millions of things to do. Every block, every alley, every chapel, every door, every brick on the streets is history. You probably can't experience it all in a whole lifetime, much less a few hours or a day. Whenever visitors to Villa Delia go to to Florence for the day, they tell me they simply have to go back. If you plan on visiting, I suggest that you stay a few days. On the first day, poke around with no agenda but to feel the local energy. It can be frustrating to get around, and the sheer volume of things to see can be intimidating, but if you're not rushed and tightly focused, you'll probably enjoy yourself more. After that first day, I leave you with all of the guidebooks to help you find what you're looking for in this glorious Renaissance city.

Don't miss Florence or its food. Have fun. Maybe I'll see you there.

A trippa *stand in Florence.*

TUSCAN BRAISED BEEF

As this meat cooks, the vegetables, broth and wine intermingle in a rich and elegant sauce. Because the flavours concentrate so much, I cook with a good wine religiously. A full-bodied Barolo or Brunello works well here or, as Tony suggests, a Rosso di Montalcino. Serve the meat with mashed or boiled tomatoes and steamed vegetables such as carrots or turnips.

INGREDIENTS

one 2 lb [1 kg]	top round roast of beef
3 oz [90 g]	pancetta or salt pork
	salt
	freshly ground black pepper
2/3 cup [150 mL]	extra virgin olive oil
1	medium onion, finely chopped
1	carrot, finely chopped
1 stalk	celery with leaves, finely chopped
2 cloves	garlic, chopped
2 cups [500 mL]	dry red wine
1 lb [500 g]	ripe tomatoes, skinned and chopped OR one 19 oz [540 mL] can, drained
4 cups [1 L]	classic meat broth *(see page 159)* or chicken stock, as needed

SERVES 6

PREPARATION

With a small knife, make deep, narrow incisions all over the roast. Cut the pancetta in thin strips and toss with salt and pepper. Insert the strips into the incisions in the meat. The pancetta adds flavour to this lean meat and keeps it from drying out.

Heat the olive oil over medium heat in a large, heavy pot or Dutch oven. Add the onion, carrot, celery and garlic and sweat them for 2 to 3 minutes until they are softened somewhat. Add the roast to the pot and brown on all sides. Add the wine and cook, still turning the roast, until the wine is almost completely evaporated.

Add the chopped tomatoes along with 1 cup [250 mL] of the broth. Cover the pot and cook over medium heat for 45 minutes, then reduce the heat to low and cook another 2 hours. Turn the roast from time to time, and add more broth as needed. You will want to keep 1/2 in. [1 cm] of broth in the pot at all times.

When you remove the pot from the heat, let it rest, covered, for 30 minutes.

Remove roast to a carving board and check the sauce. If the pot is dry, add a bit more broth and stir up the browned bits until you have a thick, syrupy sauce.

Slice the beef into serving portions and place on a warmed serving platter, drizzled with the sauce.

RECOMMENDED WINE
Rosso di Montalcino
RECOMMENDED PRODUCERS
Castello Banfi, Barbi, Il Poggione, Val di Suga
Rossi di Montalcino is less expensive and friendlier than its big brother, Brunello. Fruit-driven and gutsy, it's the perfect match for this classic Tuscan dish.

SPRING LAMB

For a few weeks in springtime, groups of city dwellers flock to the Tuscan countryside, block up all the roads with traffic and overrun the restaurants. This annual outing, la scampagnata, *coincides with the arrival of spring lamb and wild asparagus. The lamb is served in the middle of the table and people eat it with their hands – a nice, communal way to welcome the season of plenty.* Buona Pasqua: *Happy Easter.*

INGREDIENTS

2 1/2 lb [1.2 kg]	whole leg of lamb, cut by the butcher into 8 chunks with bone attached
2 cloves	garlic
1 branch	rosemary
	handful of sage
	handful of thyme
	salt
	freshly ground pepper
	extra virgin olive oil
1/2 cup [125 mL]	red wine vinegar
2 cups [500 mL]	classic meat broth *(see page 159)* or chicken stock, as needed

SERVES 6

PREPARATION

Heat a large unoiled pot over medium-high heat. Place the lamb chunks in the pot so that each piece is touching the bottom of the pot. Sweat the meat uncovered for 20 minutes.

Mince the garlic, rosemary, sage and thyme together. Once the lamb has picked up some colour, spread the herb mixture over the meat.

Reduce the heat to medium-low. Add the salt and pepper, oil and vinegar. Cook for 4 to 5 minutes, until the vinegar has evaporated. Add 1 cup [250 mL] of the broth. Cover and simmer for 1 hour. Check periodically to see if the pot is going dry, and add more broth as needed. You're not trying to create a sauce, just to keep the meat moist.

When the meat is tender, transfer it to a warmed platter and serve.

RECOMMENDED WINE
Carmignano
RECOMMENDED PRODUCERS
Fattoria Ambra, Bacchereto, Tenuta di Capezzana, Le Farnete, Iolanda Pratesi, Villa di Trefiano

The secret to Carmignano is the 10 to 15 per cent of Cabernet, both Sauvignon and Franc, in the blend. This added richness allows it to stand up to the powerful flavours of the lamb.

ROAST LEG OF LAMB

The sheep of Tuscany dine well. In among the grasses they eat are all kinds of wild herbs, and these flavour the meat. The French are very proud of the lambs they call pré-salé, *or pre-salted, which live in salt meadows. Maybe we should call our Tuscan lambs* pré-herbé.

INGREDIENTS

1	leg of lamb, bone in, approximately 4–5 lb [1–2.2 kg]
2 cloves	garlic
	salt
	freshly ground black pepper
2 lbs [1 kg]	medium potatoes, peeled and quartered lengthwise
	juice of 1 lemon
2	large onions, thinly sliced
2 cups [500 mL]	chopped, peeled tomatoes
2	bay leaves
2 sprigs	fresh oregano OR 1 tsp [5 mL] dried oregano
	small piece of cinnamon stick, broken
2 Tbsp [25 mL]	butter
1 cup [250 mL]	classic meat broth *(see page 159)* or water
1/2 cup [125 mL]	white wine

SERVES 6 TO 8

PREPARATION

Preheat the oven to 375°F [190°C].

Trim the fat from the leg of lamb. Cut the garlic in slivers. Make slits all over the lamb with the point of a knife and insert a garlic sliver in each slit. Season the lamb generously with salt and pepper. Place the lamb in a large roasting pan, leaving room to accommodate the potatoes. Roast for 45 minutes.

Arrange the potatoes around the lamb in the roasting pan. Sprinkle them with lemon juice, salt and pepper.
Top the potatoes with the onions and tomatoes. Add the bay leaves, oregano and cinnamon. Dot the vegetables with butter and add the broth and wine.

Return the pan to the oven and roast for a further 45 minutes, turning the lamb occasionally so it will brown evenly. At this point the lamb should be rare. Roast it longer if you prefer it medium or well done. When the lamb is roasted to your liking, transfer it to a carving board or platter and keep it warm. Let it rest for at least 10 minutes before you carve it.

Test the potatoes. If necessary, roast them longer. When they are tender, carve the lamb. Serve it with the potatoes, tomatoes and onions on the side.

RECOMMENDED WINE
Brunello di Montalcino
RECOMMENDED PRODUCERS
Castello Banfi, Barbi, Biondi-Santi, Ciacci Piccolomini d'Aragona, Frescobaldi, Col d'Orcia

Nothing could complement a robust meat dish like this better than the equally robust Brunello di Montalcino. Lean yet concentrated, it plays off against the sweetness of the meat.

Coscia d'agnello alla maremmana

BRAISED LEG OF LAMB FROM SOUTHERN TUSCANY

The plateau of Maremma, with its moist soil and abundant grass, is ideal sheep country. Many of the shepherds there came from Sardinia, where grass is scarce. Traditionally, Sardinian shepherds are considered the most knowledgeable about raising sheep, and thanks to their knowledge and Maremma's good grass, the lamb from there is tasty and juicy.

INGREDIENTS

one 8 lb [3.5 kg]	leg of lamb
	salt
	freshly ground black pepper
4 cloves	garlic
4	sage leaves
4 sprigs	rosemary
1/2 cup [125 mL]	olive oil
2 lbs [1 kg]	peeled and seeded tomatoes, finely chopped
2 Tbsp [25 mL]	red wine vinegar
2 cups [500 mL]	water
1 cup [250 mL]	dry red wine
2 lbs [1 kg]	fresh shelled peas

SERVES 6 TO 8

PREPARATION

Generously rub the leg of lamb with salt and pepper. Make 4 slits in the meat and insert a garlic clove, sage leaf and rosemary sprig into each one.

Heat the oil over high heat in a heavy pot that is large enough to accommodate the lamb. Brown the lamb all over. Add the tomatoes, vinegar, water and wine, and bring to a boil. Reduce the heat to low and simmer covered for about 2 hours, or until the lamb is easily pierced with a fork. Remember to turn the lamb a few times during the cooking.

Bring a large pot of salted water to a boil and add the peas. Cook them for 4 to 6 minutes or until they are tender. Drain them and add to the lamb pot for the last 10 minutes of cooking.

Carve the lamb. Arrange the slices on a platter and pour the sauce with the peas over top.

RECOMMENDED WINE
Sangiovese/Cabernet Sauvignon blends
RECOMMENDED PRODUCERS
Castello di Querceto (La Querciolaia), Frescobaldi (Mormoreto), Querciabella (Camartina), Terrabianca (Campaccio)

Cabernet Sauvignon stands up to lamb, and when blended with Sangiovese it sheds its overpowering tannins for a touch of earth and elegance. This wine is down home but stylish, and perfect for this dish.

SAUSAGES WITH LENTILS

If you are served this dish some winter evening in a Tuscan home, it means you're a welcome and honoured guest. A lot of sweat and hard work went into making it: the sausages are homemade, the lentils are home grown, the tomatoes were home preserved. This is the warm, generous spirit of genuine Tuscan hospitality.

INGREDIENTS

1 cup [250 mL]	brown lentils
2 Tbsp [25 mL]	olive oil
1/2 cup [125 mL]	prosciutto, diced
1	large onion, finely chopped
1/2 cup [125 mL]	chopped, trimmed leek
1/2 cup [125 mL]	dry white wine
1 sprig	fresh oregano, chopped
2 cloves	garlic, finely chopped
1 cup [250 mL]	peeled and diced plum tomatoes
3 cups [750 mL]	vegetable broth or chicken stock
8	Italian sausages, uncooked
	salt
	crushed black pepper

SERVES 4

PREPARATION

Cover the lentils with cold water and soak them for 2 hours.

Heat the olive oil in a large skillet over medium heat. Sauté the prosciutto for 3 to 4 minutes, then add the onion and leek, cooking them until they are browned. Add the wine, oregano and garlic.

Drain the lentils and add them to the mixture. Stir in the broth or stock. Reduce the heat to low and cook uncovered for 30 minutes. If the lentils become dry, add a bit of water.

Cook the sausages in a skillet or on a grill until they are half-cooked. Add them to the lentils, cover the pan and cook for a further 10 minutes. Adjust the seasonings with salt and pepper. Serve 2 sausages per person with the lentils on top.

RECOMMENDED WINE
Morellino di Scansano
RECOMMENDED PRODUCERS
Banti, Cecchi, Le Pupille, Motta, Moris Farms

From the mystical land of legends they call Maremma comes Morellino, a soft, voluptuous red wine. With a full-bodied dish like sausages and lentils, need I say more?

WILD HARE STEW

No Tuscan considers life worth living without at least one meal of wild hare a year. If there aren't any wild hares around, this recipe also works with rabbit or any wild meat. Mamma Delia learned from her mother to thicken hare stew with blood, but here flour does the job.

INGREDIENTS

one 6 lb [2.7 kg]	hare, cleaned and cut in 8 pieces
	salt
	freshly ground black pepper
3 Tbsp [45 mL]	flour
4 Tbsp [60 mL]	butter
3	onions, finely sliced
1 cup [250 mL]	Chianti or other dry red wine, boiling
1/3 cup [75 mL]	red wine vinegar
2 Tbsp [30 mL]	brown sugar
3 sprigs	parsley
3 sprigs	fresh thyme
1	fresh bay leaf
1/2 cup [125 mL]	classic meat broth *(see page 159)* or chicken stock, as needed
1	hare or rabbit liver, chopped
1/3 cup [75 mL]	wild mushrooms, finely chopped
4 cloves	garlic, chopped
2 Tbsp [30 mL]	tomato paste

SERVES 8

PREPARATION

Dry the pieces of hare on paper towels. Season them with salt and pepper and dust them with the flour.

Melt the butter over medium heat in a large pot, and brown the hare on all sides. Add the onions and sauté them until they pick up some colour. Add the boiling wine and cook until the liquid reduces and thickens. Add the wine vinegar, brown sugar, parsley, thyme and bay leaf and reduce the heat to medium-low. Simmer uncovered for 1 hour or until the hare is tender. If the liquid starts to cook away, add a bit of broth.

Remove the meat to a warm serving platter and keep it warm.

Discard the herbs. Bring the sauce to a creamy consistency, either by thinning it with broth or chicken stock, or by reducing it further. If the sauce is too liquid, it will overcook the liver and make it taste too strong.

Add the chopped liver, mushrooms, garlic and tomato paste. Simmer uncovered over medium-low heat for 5 more minutes. Do not let the sauce boil.

To serve, pour the sauce over the hare.

RECOMMENDED WINE
Brusco dei Barbi
RECOMMENDED PRODUCER
Fattoria dei Barbi

Some grapes grown for the great Brunello di Montalcino end up as Brusco dei Barbi. The ancient Tuscan technique, *governo*, initiates a second fermentation making this big red softer, fruitier and easier to drink sooner. Just the ticket for wild hare.

VENISON WITH ROSEMARY, SAGE AND CHERRY CRUST

Dried fruit and meat seem perfectly suited to winter, and they have been combined in Tuscan cooking since mediaeval times. This luxurious dish is popular around Christmas. Consider serving it with lots of good winter vegetables: mashed or roasted potatoes, braised red cabbage, steamed turnips or a gratinée of fennel.

INGREDIENTS

1/2 cup [125 mL]	dried cherries
1 cup [250 mL]	port
	salt
	freshly ground black pepper
1 sprig	sage, stem removed
1 sprig	rosemary, stem removed
2 Tbsp [25 mL]	olive oil
one 4-chop rack	venison (2–2 1/2 lbs [1–1.2 kg]), chine bone cut through
1	onion, skin on
1	carrot, skin on
1/2 cup [125 mL]	dry red wine
1/2 cup [125 mL]	warm water

SERVES 4

RECOMMENDED WINE
Carmignano Riserva
RECOMMENDED PRODUCERS
Fattoria Ambra, Bacchereto, Tenuta di Capezzana, Le Farnete, Iolanda Pratesi, Villa di Trefiano
Carmignano's 10 to 15 per cent cabernet gives it the body to stand up to the powerful flavours of venison.

PREPARATION

Combine the cherries, port and salt and pepper in a small pot, and simmer uncovered until the cherries are soft and the liquid is well reduced – nearly gone. Remove the mixture from the heat and allow it to cool.

Add the sage and rosemary leaves, and purée the mixture in a food processor until it forms a thick paste.

Preheat the oven to 375°F [190°C].

Heat the olive oil in a skillet over medium heat. Season the venison with salt and pepper, then sear it until it is browned on all sides.

Smear the cherry paste over the meat. Set the venison in an oiled roasting pan, bone side down. Cut the onion and carrot in half and lay them cut side down in the roasting pan. Roast the venison for 20 minutes.

Pour the wine into the roasting pan. Roast for another 10 minutes for rare, or until it has reached the preferred doneness. Remove the venison to a warmed serving platter and keep it warm.

Put the roasting pan on top of the stove over medium-high heat, and add the 1/2 cup [125 mL] of warm water to the pan juices, scraping up the browned bits with a wooden spatula. Bring the juices to a boil and boil for 1 or 2 minutes, or until reduced to a silky consistency.

To serve, cut the rack into chops. Strain the juices and spoon them over the chops.

Cinghiale in umido

DRUNKEN WILD BOAR

Wild boar was a major part of the Etruscans' diet, and today's Tuscans still have a taste for it. This rich stew ends up with just enough flavourful, concentrated sauce to coat each piece of meat. It works equally well with wild boar, pork or venison. A plain starch like polenta or wide noodles is a nice counterpoint.

INGREDIENTS

1 1/2 lbs [750 g]	lean wild boar, pork or venison, cut into 2 in. [5 cm] cubes
1/2 cup [125 mL]	extra virgin olive oil
1	onion, finely chopped
1 stalk	celery with leaves, finely chopped
2 cloves	garlic, finely chopped
	handful of parsley, chopped
1 branch	rosemary
	handful of sage leaves
2 cups [500 mL]	classic meat broth *(see page 159)*, or chicken or beef stock
2 cups [500 mL]	dry red wine
1 can	tomato paste (5 1/2 oz [156 mL])
4	bay leaves
3/4 cup [175 mL]	black olives
	salt
	freshly ground black pepper

SERVES 4

PREPARATION

In a large, dry sauté pan, sweat the meat over medium heat for 3 to 4 minutes, until the liquid evaporates and the meat starts to brown. This method takes away any gamey smell, and it works for all wild meat.

Add the oil. Stir in the onion, celery, garlic, parsley, rosemary and sage. Reduce the heat to low and cook covered for 30 minutes. Stir it occasionally.

Add 1 cup [250 mL] of the broth. Cover and cook another 30 minutes, stirring occasionally.

Add the wine and increase the heat to high. Cook uncovered for 3 to 4 minutes. Stir in the tomato paste, bay leaves, olives and remaining 1 cup [250 mL] of the broth. Add salt and pepper. Reduce the heat to low, cover the pan and cook for another 30 minutes, stirring occasionally.

RECOMMENDED WINE
SuperTuscan Red
RECOMMENDED PRODUCERS
Antinori (Tignanello), Rocca delle Macìe (Roccato), Ruffino (Il Borgo), San Felice (Vigorello), Umberto Villa Delia (Bambolo)

These are Tuscany's biggest and richest reds, with the power and structure to tame most wild dishes.

DESSERTS

*As the Tuscans have a sweet tooth, we have a sweet approach to life.
We just don't want to leave the table, so fruit, cheese
and a tart provide an excuse to linger.*

Every town and village has a festival to celebrate what grows best there. This is the cherry festival in Lari.

ALMOND BISCOTTI

Nine out of ten times, when you are visiting someone's home in Tuscany, you will be presented with a glass of Vin Santo and some biscotti as a gesture of welcome. This is one of the highest compliments you can receive, because both the wine and the biscotti are usually made by the hosts, and it's always polite not to refuse them.

INGREDIENTS

7 cups [1.75 L]	flour
5	eggs (save 1 egg for egg wash)
1 3/4 cups [425 mL]	sugar
1 cup [250 mL]	unsalted butter (2 sticks), room temperature
2 tsp [10 mL]	baking soda
3/4 cup + 1 Tbsp [190 mL]	Marsala or Vin Santo
	pinch of salt
1 cup [250 mL]	whole almonds with skin

MAKES 40 TO 50 BISCOTTI

PREPARATION

Pour the flour onto a clean surface and make a well in the middle. Put 4 eggs, sugar, butter, baking soda, wine, salt and almonds into the well, one at a time. Incorporate the flour by hand into the other ingredients, a little at a time. When you have a firm dough, you can stop incorporating flour. Form it into a ball and let it rest for 30 minutes covered with a clean cloth. If it starts to flatten out, put it in the fridge so it will retain its shape.

Preheat oven to 350°F [170°C].

Divide the dough into 3 pieces, and shape it like baguettes. Each one should be about 3 in. wide and 2 in. thick [7.5 x 5 cm]. Space them out on one or two baking sheets. Beat the remaining egg and brush the egg wash over the tops.

Bake for 15 minutes at 350°F [180°C], then remove them from the oven and reduce the temperature to 225°F [105°C].

Cut the rolls on the diagonal into 1 in. [2.5 cm] slices, and arrange the slices on their sides on baking sheets. Return to the oven. Bake about 1 hour, until nice and dry and golden brown. Allow the biscotti to cool to room temperature, then store them in an airtight container.

RECOMMENDED WINE
Vin Santo
RECOMMENDED PRODUCERS
Antinori, Brolio, Frescobaldi
Tuscan residents love to sip aromatic Vin Santo with biscotti or an assortment of cakes. Depending upon your preference you can choose among sweet, semisweet or dry wines.

VIN SANTO

Piero Antinori says "Vin Santo, also known as Vino Santo, has been made in Tuscany since at least mediaeval times, and was probably named 'holy wine' because of its use during the Mass." Tuscan Vin Santo is almost always best served as a dessert wine.

A blend of mostly Trebbiano with some Malvasia, it has an enticing amber colour, a honeysuckle nose and full, rich flavours.

Both sweet and complex, it is thought to be the perfect accompaniment to twice-baked biscotti.

The production of Vin Santo is unique. Each year wineries pick grapes at various times during the harvest to ensure a mix of high acid, high sugar and perfectly balanced grapes. The grapes are then spread by hand on special straw mats in large, airy lofts and left to dry until the end of the year when they are pressed.

The must is then transferred into small 50- to 200- litre oak casks where a long, slow alcoholic fermentation takes place. When the wine reaches 15 to 16 degrees alcohol, the fermentation quits and the wine remains in cask for another three years.

TUSCAN RING CAKE

This dense cake was one of my mother's specialties, and it was good any time of day. It is meant to stand up to dipping in coffee or being spread with jam, which is how we ate it in the morning. For dessert Mamma dressed it up with different syrups, sauces or fruits. Be sure to use instant yeast, otherwise it won't rise.

INGREDIENTS

5	eggs
1 1/2 cups [375 mL]	sugar
1/2 cup [125 mL]	unsalted butter (1 stick), at room temperature
3 1/2 cups [875 mL]	flour
1 envelope	instant dry yeast (1 Tbsp [15 mL])
1/2 cup [125 mL]	milk
1/2 cup [125 mL]	Vin Santo or other sweet white wine
	zest of 1 lemon
	pinch of salt

SERVES 6

PREPARATION

Gently whisk the eggs and sugar together in a large bowl.

In a separate bowl, work the butter into the flour with your fingers until it is all incorporated. Without mixing, add the yeast, milk, wine, zest and salt. Pour the contents of this bowl into the egg mixture. Stir well with a wooden spoon.

Your batter will be thick, like a moist bread dough. Mix it well, without incorporating too much air. Don't worry about any small lumps.

Grease a tube pan or Bundt pan and dust it with flour. Spoon in the batter.

Preheat the oven to 325°F [160°C].

Bake for 40 minutes or until a toothpick comes out clean. Let the cake cool to room temperature before you remove it from the pan.

CHICKPEA PANCAKE

Around the Pisa area, when a mother picks up her children from school, they'll often stop for a piece of cecina to give everybody a mid-afternoon energy boost.

INGREDIENTS

4 cups [1 L]	cold water
2 cups [500 mL]	chickpea flour
1 cup [250 mL]	extra virgin olive oil
	pinch of salt
	freshly ground white pepper

SERVES 6

PREPARATION

Whisk together cold water and flour until there are no lumps. The liquid will be very starchy. Add the oil and salt, and whisk again until they are incorporated. Let the mixture rest at least 30 minutes.

Preheat the oven to 450°F [230°C].

Generously oil a 14 in. [35 cm] round, rimmed pizza pan (not the kind with holes!) or a large rimmed baking sheet. Pour in the batter and bake for about 40 minutes, or until the crust is a little crispy on top.

Remove the pancake from the oven and let it rest for 5 minutes.
Cut it into wedges and dust with white pepper.

A Tuscan Christmas

I remember Christmas as a religious holiday. Most of the activities were centred on church, so discipline and respect went along with the fun. It was not so much a food holiday ... but we still ate well. This was Tuscany, after all.

OUR MOST IMPORTANT MEAL came on Christmas Eve. It was a quiet dinner with close family only, just the people who lived in the house, followed by midnight Mass. It was also the most precise meal. We had the same dishes every year, and many of them were served only on this night.

Christmas Eve is called *la vigilia*, the vigil or fast. And here is how we would fast. The first course was a giant pot of vegetable broth with little ravioli floating in it. In my house the raviolini were stuffed with breadcrumbs, carrots, onions, lemon zest, nutmeg and Parmesan cheese. Some other regions stuff them with artichokes, spinach or squash.

The second course featured saltwater and freshwater fish. Salt cod, *baccala*, came with a simple tomato sauce. (Marietta's salt cod recipe is on page 95.) We also ate *capitone in umido*, large freshwater eels cut in thick slices, floured, pan fried and finished in a coulis of tomato with raisins and browned onions. Oh boy, they were delicious.

Our fast continued with tiny clams steamed with parsley, garlic, lemon and white wine. As soon as they opened, they were tossed with spaghettini or linguine and blessed with some black pepper.

The final dish was a whole steamed cauliflower sprinkled with a mixture of breadcrumbs, garlic, hard-cooked eggs, anchovies and parsley and served with a sprinkle of lemon. *Mamma mia*, it was so good I could hardly stand it. I hated cauliflower and I hated anchovies, but I loved this.

As you can see, our fast was not a terrible deprivation, just a meatless meal that would keep us going through midnight Mass and prepare our appetites for the enormous lunch that followed the next day.

On Christmas Day, more family, more fun, more food – everything we had denied ourselves the night before. Lunch was a feast of courses: antipasti; soup; pasta; fried vegetables like carrots, tomatoes, cauliflower (see page 19), artichokes and potatoes; steamed or grilled calamari, red mullet, prawns and other fish; bollito misto (see page 119); and finally, arrosto platters of grilled or roasted meat including pork ribs, veal chops, beefsteak (see page 123) and sausages, along with grilled vegetables.

It was a tradition for my father, with a big smile, to bring to the table the first bottles of wine from the year's harvest. Everybody was eager to taste the new vintage. I remember such talking and laughing, such cheering and teasing – I don't recall any other occasion when so much food and so much happiness were shared around the table. Even we kids were allowed to be noisy and a bit cheeky – maybe even to say bad words, which we could never get away with on any other day.

Traditionally my brother and sisters and I each wrote a note to our parents saying how much we loved them and making promises to be good, to study hard, to help around the house for the rest of the year. The notes would be placed on the table under their plates, and when the first course was taken away, there they would be! In return for the notes, we hoped to receive a nice gift on Epiphany: the more flowery the note, the greater the gift we expected.

These are great memories I will treasure forever. I hope I can pass on these wonderful experiences to my own son, and I wish the same joy to you in your own celebrations. *Buon Natale.*

Sweet Ricotta Cake

As with everything else in Tuscany, ricotta cheese has its season. It is usually produced in the spring when the sheep give their best milk. That's why it is associated with Easter. This afternoon treat is served warm or cold with tea or coffee – or spumante if there's something to celebrate.

Ingredients

2 lbs [1 kg]	ricotta cheese (two 500 g containers)
3/4 cup [175 mL]	sugar
	pinch of salt
1/2 cup [125 mL]	fine dry breadcrumbs
4	eggs
1/4 cup [50 mL]	grated unsweetened chocolate
	icing sugar for garnish
	sprigs of mint for garnish

Serves 6 to 8

Preparation

Combine the ricotta, sugar and salt in a bowl and mix well. Chill the mixture overnight in the refrigerator in order for it to become fluffy and moist. This overnight rest also takes the bite out of the ricotta and makes it mild and sweet.

Next day, preheat the oven to 350°F [180°C]. Grease an 8 in. [20 cm] round baking dish and dust the inside with the breadcrumbs.

Stir together the eggs and chocolate and combine with the ricotta. Transfer the mixture to the prepared baking dish and bake uncovered for about 1 hour, or until the cake is firm.

To serve, slice the cake into wedges or scoop it onto a plate. Dust with icing sugar and decorate the plate with mint sprigs or a fruit coulis.

MASCARPONE MOUSSE

We had few desserts when I was growing up, but this one was a favourite because the ingredients were always around the house. It is a very aristocratic dessert with a smooth, pleasing texture. It is fine on its own or with some fresh strawberries in season.

INGREDIENTS

	juice of 1 large orange
1/2 cup [125 mL]	orange liqueur
4	whole amaretti (Italian almond macaroons)
2	eggs, separated
1/2 lb [250 g]	mascarpone cheese
3 oz [90 g]	unsweetened chocolate (3 squares), shaved
3/4 cup [175 mL]	sugar

SERVES 4

PREPARATION

Squeeze the orange juice into a bowl and add the orange liqueur. Quickly dip the cookies into the orange mixture so they soak up some liquid. Put each cookie in the bottom of a large stemmed glass.

In another bowl, stir the egg yolks and mascarpone together until smooth. Don't beat the mixture. Stir in the shaved chocolate.

In a third bowl, beat the egg whites with sugar to the soft peak stage. Fold the whites into the mascarpone mixture.

Pour the mousse over the amaretti in the stemmed glasses. Refrigerate for two or more hours before serving.

CITRUS CREAM WITH MINT

The mint sprinkled on top gives a fresh lift to the creamy richness of the dessert.

INGREDIENTS

1 cup [250 mL]	whole milk
	zest of 1/2 orange
	zest of 1/2 lemon
1/4	vanilla bean
	OR 1/2 tsp [2 mL] vanilla extract
1	whole clove
2 Tbsp [30 mL]	sugar
1 Tbsp [15 mL]	powdered gelatin
1 cup [250 mL]	whipping cream
	lemon rind for garnish
	chopped fresh mint for garnish

SERVES 4

PREPARATION

In a small, heavy pot, combine the milk, zests, vanilla, clove and sugar. Bring the mixture to a low boil and cook uncovered for approximately 10 minutes.

Strain the liquid into a cold mixing bowl. Add the gelatin and stir; this will allow the gelatin to dissolve in the warm mixture and eventually to solidify.

Once the gelatin has dissolved, add the whipping cream. Using an electric beater or a whisk, whip the mixture until it thickens. You're trying to get a silky thickness rather than a stiff whipped cream texture. Transfer the cream to four 3 in. [12 mL] individual serving ramekins. Place the ramekins in the refrigerator and allow them to chill for at least 4 hours.

To unmold, jiggle the top a bit to loosen it from the sides, then upend the ramekins onto plates. Garnish with lemon rind and mint.

TIRAMISU

Mamma Delia was known in the neighbourhood for making the best tiramisù. When it was cooling in the fridge, we kids would sneak in and sample it by sticking our fingers in it. By the time the tiramisù was ready it would look like Swiss cheese. "Aha," Mom would say, "little mouths went into the tray." And she could always tell whose fingers made the holes.

INGREDIENTS

3	eggs
3 Tbsp [45 mL]	sugar
1 1/4 cups [300 mL]	mascarpone cheese
1/3 cup [75 mL]	fresh espresso, cooled
1/4 cup [60 mL]	Cognac
1 large package	ladyfingers (5 oz [150 g])
	cocoa powder for dusting

SERVES 6

PREPARATION

Separate the eggs into two medium bowls. With an electric mixer, beat the whites with the sugar until stiff peaks form. In the other bowl, use the mixer to cream the yolks and mascarpone to a rich, smooth consistency. Fold the cheese mixture delicately into the whites.

Stir the espresso and the Cognac together in a flat-bottomed dish and dip the ladyfingers quickly into the liquid, one at a time. The secret is to allow them to absorb a bit of the liquid but not so much that they fall apart.

Place the dipped ladyfingers in a layer in an 8 in. [2 L] square glass baking dish. Spread 1/3 of the mascarpone mixture over the ladyfingers to the same thickness. Repeat the process with two more layers of ladyfingers and filling, ending with the mascarpone mixture. Dust the top with cocoa powder.

Refrigerate for at least 2 hours before serving. In fact, tiramisu is best served the next day. It can also be frozen, then thawed for a couple of hours before serving.

FIGS IN SYRUP

By December, the autumn figs are nicely dried and ready to eat. They're delicious on their own, but I think they're even better stewed this way. This is a great winter dessert.

INGREDIENTS

1 lb [500 g]	dried figs
2 cups [500 mL]	water
1 cup [250 mL]	whole blanched almonds
1/2 cup [125 mL]	sugar
1/2 cup [125 mL]	honey
1	lemon
1/2 cup [125 mL]	chopped pistachios for garnish
1 cup [250 mL]	whipping cream or ice cream for garnish

SERVES 6

PREPARATION

Soak the figs in the water for 8 hours. Remove the figs from the water and transfer the water to a pot. Insert an almond into each fig through the bottom.

Add the sugar to the soaking water, and heat, stirring constantly until the sugar is dissolved. Add the honey.

With a vegetable peeler, remove the yellow zest from the lemon in strips. Add the zest to the pan and squeeze in the juice of the lemon. Bring the liquid to a boil.

Add the figs and simmer uncovered for about 30 minutes or until you have a syrup. Remove the lemon zest.

Arrange the figs upright in a bowl and pour the syrup over. Allow the figs to come to room temperature, then cover and chill.

To serve, sprinkle the figs with chopped pistachios, and add a spoonful of whipping cream or ice cream if you wish.

QUICK SWEET CHESTNUT FRITTERS

*Mmm, mmm, mmm. I still remember the taste of these on a cold winter day.
I would rush home from school and before I got to the door I could smell
the oil, hot and ready for frying. Chestnuts, in all their forms, add flavour to the
Tuscan winter. You will find chestnut flour in Italian markets and specialty
food stores.*

INGREDIENTS

1 cup [250 mL]	chestnut flour
1 cup [250 mL]	water, room temperature
2 Tbsp [30 mL]	sugar
	olive oil for frying
	icing sugar for dusting

SERVES 4

PREPARATION

In a bowl, mix the flour, water and sugar until it forms a dense paste. Pour 1 in. [2.5 cm] of oil into a small skillet and heat over medium-high heat.

Drop tablespoons of paste into the oil, being careful not to add too many at one time. The oil should bubble vigorously around them. Fry until they are golden brown on one side, then turn them over and brown the other side.

Remove the fritters from the oil using a slotted spoon, and place them on paper towels to drain. Sprinkle some icing sugar over the top and serve.

GRANDMOTHER'S PINE NUT TART

Everybody's grandma makes this quick, simple dessert and, naturally, everybody's grandma claims to make the very best. They also pass the skill on to their grandchildren. Kids practise on this tart, under Nonna's watchful eye, when they're learning to cook. I have vivid memories of cooking this tart when I was eight.

INGREDIENTS

PASTRY

2 cups [500 mL]	flour
2	whole eggs
1	egg yolk
1/2 cup [125 mL]	sugar
1/2 cup [125 mL]	unsalted butter (1 stick), at room temperature
	pinch of salt

PINE NUT FILLING

1 3/4 cup [425 mL]	whole milk
4	egg yolks
1/2 cup [125 mL]	sugar
2 Tbsp [25 mL]	flour
3/4 cup [175 mL]	pine nuts (100 g package), not toasted
1 Tbsp [15 mL]	icing sugar for garnish

MAKES ONE 10 IN. [25 CM] TART

PREPARATION

For the pastry, pour flour onto a clean work surface and make a well in the middle. Put the whole eggs, yolk, sugar, butter and salt in the well. Keeping a ring of flour on the outside, work the ingredients with your hands into a dough that is about the same consistency as for refrigerator cookies. Depending on the moisture in the air, the age of the flour and other factors, you are unlikely to need all the flour.

Shape the dough into a ball, cover and let it rest in the fridge for at least 30 minutes. Meanwhile, make the filling.

Heat the milk just to the boiling point over medium-low heat. In a bowl, combine the egg yolks with the sugar and flour, stirring until the mixture turns pale. Stir the hot milk into the egg mixture, a bit at a time. The mixture will become thick and creamy. Cool the filling to room temperature.

Preheat the oven to 350°F [180°C].

To assemble, roll out the dough on a floured board to about 1/4 in. [5 mm] thickness. Curl it onto the rolling pin and transfer it to a 10 in. [25 cm] tart pan. Gently push the dough into the contours of the pan and up the sides so it rises just above the rim. Because of the cookie-dough consistency, you can easily patch any cracks or tears.

Pour the cooled egg mixture into the dough. Sprinkle pine nuts evenly over the top. Bake for 40 to 50 minutes, until the filling is solid and golden, with dark spots.

To serve, place wedges on plates and sprinkle icing sugar through a fine-meshed strainer over top.

A Day in Tuscany

As much as things have changed since I grew up, the Tuscan day still generally follows the traditional rhythms set by the signori della terra, *the gentlemen of the land. I don't like to call them farmers, because that word doesn't convey the great respect that Tuscans have for the people who grow their food. The signori are considered rich, even if they have no money, because they look after and protect the land.*

THEIR DAY STARTS with the sunrise, and their meals are spaced about three hours apart to provide an energy boost whenever it's needed. Although the rest of us don't rise as early or work as hard, we still space our meals in the same way.

The day starts with a hearty Tuscan breakfast – *caffè e latte*: coffee with milk. And maybe a slice of bread to dip in it. I always get a kick out of the surprise on some people's faces when they find out that we don't eat breakfast.

The real eating begins at about ten o'clock when everybody heads to the local bar for an espresso and a pastry. For the signori, who have been working in the fields for four hours by now, this mid-morning break is no snack; it's the first solid food of the day, so it will be something substantial, such as a piece of cold frittata or some prosciutto.

Around one o'clock, Tuscan working life stops for lunch. The stores and workshops close, restaurants and bars fill up, the signori go home from the fields. Everybody enjoys a big meal and a little rest afterwards. It's a good thing that none of our invaders ever figured this out. They could have marched in and taken over, and nobody in Tuscany would have noticed until hours later. Lunchtime is changing in the cities because of the demands of modern business and the needs of tourists, but the farther you get into the countryside, the more you'll see the traditional respect for the most important meal of the day.

The next opportunity to eat comes in the late afternoon. It's called *merenda*, and consists of something a little bit sweet and starchy, like chestnut fritters (*see page 150*) or a chickpea pancake (*see page 143*). It's mostly the signori and the bambini just home from school who eat this snack.

I remember looking forward to it eagerly, and I still see kids rushing home with big smiles, knowing there's a treat waiting.

At the end of the work day, the parade starts – and it's definitely not a rush hour. *Passeggiata* is a time for walking around, greeting friends and catching up on the events of the day. Boys and girls eye each other secretly, and adults discuss the latest news over a small Campari or a glass of wine.

Dinner, eaten at eight or nine o'clock, is a time for the family to relax together over a lighter meal than lunch. It tends more towards vegetables and soup, and probably includes some lunch leftovers.

If it's summer and too hot to sleep, we stretch the day with another passeggiata, and catch up on what everybody else had for dinner.

It may seem that we Tuscans eat often, but the point is, we never walk, work or drive while we eat. We don't eat just for something to do. When it's time for food, we sit down so our bodies' energy can concentrate on digesting. Outside the cities, it is tough to find a restaurant that is open between meal times. In Tuscany, we think there's a right place and a right time for everything.

ALMOND RICOTTA TART

You may be tempted to enhance this tart, but don't. It doesn't need anything except maybe a dusting of icing sugar for decoration. A sweet wine or Spumante Moscato accompanies it nicely. This is a great dessert to take to a picnic.

INGREDIENTS

PASTRY

3 1/2 cups [875 mL]	flour
1 cup [250 mL]	butter, cold (2 sticks)
1 1/4 cups [300 mL]	sugar
2	whole eggs
1	egg yolk
1	vanilla bean, ground
	OR 1/2 tsp [2 mL] vanilla extract
	pinch of salt

ALMOND RICOTTA FILLING

2 1/4 cups [550 mL]	ricotta [600 g]
1/2 cup [125 mL]	crushed amaretti (Italian almond macaroons)
1/3 cup [75 mL]	fresh espresso, cooled
1/4 cup [50 mL]	Amaretto liqueur

MAKES ONE 14 IN. [35 CM] TART

PREPARATION

Pour the flour onto a clean work surface and make a well in the middle. Fill the well with butter, sugar, whole eggs and yolk, vanilla and salt. Gently work in the flour with your hands until the dough comes together and forms a ball. You may not need all of the flour. Cover it with a clean cloth and let it rest for 15 minutes.

Preheat oven to 325°F [160°C].

Roll out the dough to fit a 14 in. [35 cm] tart pan, and press it up the sides so it is a bit higher than the rim. Some dough will be left over.

Combine ricotta, cookie crumbs, espresso and liqueur in a bowl and fold the ingredients together with a wooden spoon. Add the filling to the pastry shell. Make strips or shapes with the leftover dough and decorate the top. Bake for 40 minutes, or until golden brown.

Apple Tart

Merenda is the afternoon snack in Italy – a quick something to boost energy and provide a little break. This apple tart is often featured, sometimes served with a coulis of whatever fruit is in season, sometimes with whipped cream or zabaglione. Oh yes, and maybe a little Vin Santo.

Ingredients

4	eggs
1 cup [250 mL]	milk
1 3/4 cups [425 mL]	sugar
1/2 cup [125 mL]	butter (1 stick), at room temperature
1 cup [250 mL]	flour
1 tsp [5 mL]	vanilla extract
1 envelope	instant dry yeast (1 Tbsp [15 mL])
	zest of 1 lemon
1/4 cup [50 mL]	pine nuts
1/3 cup [75 g]	raisins
	pinch of salt
4	large Golden Delicious apples

Serves 6

Preparation

In a bowl, beat the eggs with the milk and sugar until smooth. Add butter, flour, vanilla, yeast, lemon zest, pine nuts, raisins and salt. When the dough is smooth and forms a ball, let it rest at room temperature for 5 minutes.

Put 2/3 of the dough in a 10 in. [25 cm] tart pan. With your fingers, spread it out from the centre until it covers the inside of the pan, with a bit sticking up above the rim.

Preheat oven to 350°F [180°C].

Peel, core and thinly slice the apples. Arrange them in layers over the dough.

Roll out the remaining dough to form a top crust. Place it over the apples and crimp the edges. Poke the top with a fork several times to allow steam to escape as it bakes.

Bake 45 minutes to 1 hour, until the crust is golden and slightly puffed.

BASICS

To a Tuscan, food is not just something to eat. It is the very core of life.

SLENDER BREADSTICKS

These will keep for a week in a breadbox, but they go so fast they probably won't last that long. Part of the secret is to use fresh yeast, which has a better taste than dried yeast and doesn't expand as much. It can be hard to find. Some well-stocked stores carry it in the frozen food section. You might be able to buy fresh yeast from a bakery as well. Keep it refrigerated or frozen until you need it, then let it come to room temperature.

INGREDIENTS

4 1/2 cups [1.25 L]	flour
2 tsp [10 mL]	sugar
2 tsp [10 mL]	salt
4 Tbsp [60 mL]	fresh yeast
1/2 cup [125 mL]	extra virgin olive oil
1 1/3 cups [325 mL]	lukewarm water
1/4 cup [60 mL]	semolina for dusting

MAKES 40 TO 60 BREADSTICKS

PREPARATION

Put all ingredients in a mixer with a dough hook and mix until they come together and form a ball.

Place the dough on an oiled surface, preferably stone. Knead briefly, until the dough is oiled but still slightly sticky. Gently stretch it and pat it flat to form a large rectangle about 1 in. [2.5 cm] thick. Fold the dough in half lengthwise, cover with a clean cloth and let it rest for 30 minutes.

Preheat the oven to 325°F [160°C].

Cut the dough crosswise into finger-width strips. Dust them lightly in semolina. Holding one end of each strip, gently pull the dough to the length of the baking sheet. Do not overwork the strips.

Place the strips on an unoiled baking sheet and bake for 30 minutes until golden brown.

CLASSIC MEAT BROTH

This fragrant stock is used in many recipes throughout the book. It's a good idea to freeze some in 1- or 2-cup containers so you can always have just what you need on hand.

INGREDIENTS

12 cups [3L]	cold water
1/2 lb [250 g]	beef, cut in large chunks
1/2 lb [250 g]	beef bones (shank and shoulder)
1/2	boiling fowl or roasting chicken plus any extra chicken bones you have on hand
1	onion, skinned and cut in half
2	large carrots
1 stalk	celery, with leaves
1	leek, cut in half lengthwise and washed
2	medium-sized ripe tomatoes
6	basil leaves
10	whole black peppercorns
	pinch of coarse salt

MAKES APPROXIMATELY
8 CUPS [2 L]

PREPARATION

Put all ingredients in a large pot and bring to a boil. Cook uncovered at a very gentle boil for 2 hours to extract all the flavour.

Remove the meat and vegetables with a strainer or slotted spoon and discard. Pour the liquid through a fine sieve lined with cheesecloth. This step will clear the broth and remove some of the fat. Allow the broth to cool at room temperature and remove any fat that rises to the top. Add salt and pepper to taste.

Pizza Crust

Pizza dough will keep for a week in a plastic bag in the refrigerator. Let it come to room temperature before you bake it or it will burn before it's cooked through. The dough will reactivate if you dust it with flour and knead it for a minute. For true Tuscan flavour, seek out fresh yeast. It tastes better and is more active than dried yeast. Fresh yeast loses its leavening power quickly, so buy it close to the time you need it and keep it frozen or refrigerated.

Ingredients

3 1/2 cups [875 mL]	flour
2 Tbsp [25 mL]	fresh yeast
1/8 tsp [0.5 mL]	salt
1 Tbsp [15 mL]	extra virgin olive oil
1 cup [250 mL]	lukewarm water

Makes five
10 in. [25 cm] crusts

Preparation

Pour the flour on a clean work surface and make a well in the middle. Add the yeast and salt. Crumble them together with your fingers, incorporating a little flour as you do so. Add the olive oil and the water, and incorporate a little more flour to form a liquid, runny base. Add more water if the base is too solid. Once you have the base, work in as much of the remaining flour as you need to form a soft dough that is not sticky. Knead the dough until it is silky smooth. (The longer you knead it, the better it gets. I like to work it for a total of about 30 minutes.)

Put the dough in a large, oiled bowl, cover it with a clean cloth and leave it in the warmest corner of the kitchen. Once it has doubled in size, anywhere from 45 minutes to 1 1/2 hours, punch it down and cut it into 5 equal balls. Place them on a baking sheet, cover with a clean cloth and let them rise again until doubled in size, 20 to 35 minutes.

Preheat the oven to 450°F [230°C]. If you have a pizza stone, put it in to heat when you start the oven.

With a rolling pin dusted with flour, roll out each ball as thin as possible (about 10 in. [25 cm] in diameter). Add your favourite toppings and seasonings and slide the pizza onto the pizza stone in the oven, or sprinkle some cornmeal on a baking sheet and slide the pizza onto that.

Bake for 6 to 10 minutes or until the crust is golden and the toppings are bubbling.

PESTO

I strongly recommend that you make your own pesto, even though you can buy it commercially. With a couple of minutes' time investment you get the fresh flavour of the Mediterranean. And there's nothing to cook: just put it directly on hot pasta, a piece of fish or into soup. Use young, firm pecorino cheese if you can find it. It is the original cheese of pesto.

INGREDIENTS

1/2 cup [125 mL]	pine nuts
1/2 cup [125 mL]	grated pecorino or Parmesan cheese
	handful of parsley
20	medium leaves basil
1 clove	garlic
	salt
	freshly ground black pepper
1/4 cup [60 mL]	extra virgin olive oil

SERVES 4

PREPARATION

Place all ingredients in a food processor and pulse until the mixture is finely chopped but not pasty.

This pesto can be frozen in self-sealing plastic bags for convenience.

RICH BEEF SAUCE

Even though there's a different recipe for every family, Italians all agree that a ragù *is a concentrate. Long, slow cooking caramelizes the flavours, extracts the depth of each ingredient and reduces the sauce to something very rich and dense, without a lot of liquid. A* ragù *can start with with meat, fish, rabbit or vegetables – anything really. The end result will be a sauce that intensifies the original aromas and flavours. It is usually served over a flat pasta like fettuccine or tagliatelle.*

INGREDIENTS

1	onion
2 cloves	garlic
1 stalk	celery
1	carrot
	handful of fresh parsley
10	fresh sage leaves
1 sprig	rosemary
10 oz [300 g]	lean ground beef
1/2 cup [125 mL]	dry white wine
2 cans	tomato paste (5 1/2 oz [300 g])
	salt
	freshly ground black pepper
2 cups [500 mL]	classic meat broth *(see page 159)*

SERVES 6

PREPARATION

Finely chop all the vegetables and herbs together. Put the finely chopped mixture and the meat into a dry sauté pan over medium heat. Cook, stirring with a wooden spoon, for 30 minutes.

Stir in wine, tomato paste, salt, pepper and broth. Cover and cook, stirring occasionally, for another 30 minutes. Taste for seasonings and adjust with salt and pepper.

TOMATO SAUCE

You can go out into the garden and gather all the ingredients for this sauce, then throw everything in a pot and cook it without sautéing anything first. Somehow this cooking method extracts all the sweetness of the ingredients. Serve it over your favourite pasta.

INGREDIENTS

2 lbs [1 kg]	ripe roma or plum tomatoes, halved
4 cloves	garlic, whole and peeled
1	small fresh hot chili, finely chopped (about 1/2 tsp [2 mL])
	small handful of fresh sage leaves
	small handful of fresh basil leaves
	pinch of coarse salt
	salt
	freshly ground black pepper
1 Tbsp [15 mL]	extra virgin olive oil

SERVES 6

PREPARATION

Put the tomatoes, garlic cloves, chili, sage, basil and coarse salt into a large pot. Boil uncovered for 30 minutes until the tomatoes are softened.

Pass the mixture through a food mill or strainer into a smaller pot. This step will remove skins, seeds and stems.

Simmer the sauce uncovered until it is reduced to a creamy consistency. Adjust the seasonings with salt and pepper, and stir in the extra virgin olive oil.

HOMEMADE WINE VINEGAR

If you have a lot of wine around, you might as well make your own wine vinegar. When you make this recipe, you create the "mother," the gummy substance that causes the wine to ferment. Once you have this starter, you can simply add it to other wine to make more vinegar. For best results, use lower-alcohol dry wines that have not been pasteurized. Kosher wines have been flash-pasteurized and won't work. Homemade wines are ideal.

INGREDIENTS

5 cups [1.25 L] wine
handful of broken spaghetti

YIELDS 5 CUPS [1.25L]

PREPARATION

Pour the wine into an 8 cup [2 L], wide-mouthed glass bottle, preferably one made of dark glass. Add the spaghetti. Pasta contains the proteins and enzymes that will stimulate the fermentation.

Cover the mouth of the bottle with 4 layers of cheesecloth and secure with an elastic band. Leave the wine fermenting for 3 months in a dark place that never gets colder than 68°F [20°C]. Don't disturb the bottle during this time. The thin layer of bacteria that forms at the top of the liquid is the mother of the vinegar.

When 3 months have passed, transfer the liquid into sterilized glass bottles: remove the cheesecloth from the bottle, line a small sieve with clean cheesecloth and filter the vinegar through the sieve into new (sterilized) bottles. Hold a slotted spoon over the neck of the original container as you pour, to help separate the mother from the vinegar. Tightly close the vinegar bottles and keep them in a dark place.

Using the mother that you have separated, you can immediately start a new batch of vinegar (use the same amount of wine) or you can keep the mother in a sealed jar in a dark place until you need it. Make sure the mother never gets colder than 68°F [20°C].

INDEX